# NATIONALISM

## THE ECONOMIC STRATEGY FOR SURVIVAL OF DEVELOPING COUNTRIES

# NATIONALISM

## THE ECONOMIC STRATEGY FOR SURVIVAL OF DEVELOPING COUNTRIES

Col. Bhaskar Sarkar

ATLANTIC
PUBLISHERS & DISTRIBUTORS (P) LTD

Published by
**ATLANTIC**
**PUBLISHERS & DISTRIBUTORS (P) LTD**

7/22, Ansari Road, Darya Ganj,
New Delhi-110002
Phones : +91-11-23273880, 23275880, 23280451
Fax : +91-11-23285873
Web : www.atlanticbooks.com
E-mail : info@atlanticbooks.com

Branch Office
5, Nallathambi Street, Wallajah Road,
Chennai-600002
Phones : +91-44-64611085, 32413319
E-mail : chennai@atlanticbooks.com



ISBN 978-81-269-1093-9



Printed in India at Nice Printing Press, A-33/3A, Site-IV, Industrial Area, Sahibabad, Ghaziabad, U.P.

*Dedicated to*

His Excellency, Mr. Mahatir Mohammed, Prime Minister of Malaysia whose nationalist economic policies and courage to take on the developed world in the wake of the Asian meltdown of 1998 have inspired me to write this book

# Preface

The United States emerged after the World War II as the strongest economy in the world. It had experienced rapid industrial growth and capital accumulation during the war years. The US had remained untouched by the ravages of World War I and II and had built a thriving manufacturing industry. It had grown wealthy selling weapons and lending money to other nations fighting the war. In fact, the US industrial production in 1945 was more than double that of annual production of the total of all other countries between the pre-war years of 1935 and 1939. In contrast, Europe and East Asia were physically and economically shattered. The US held most of world's investment capital, manufacturing, production and exports. In 1945, the US produced half the world's coal and two-thirds of the world's oil. It held 80 per cent of the world's gold reserves. The US thus started with initial economic advantage after World War II and consolidated it to assume leadership of the capitalist world. It was and still is determined to perpetuate its domination of the world economy.

After the World War II, Communism and the Soviet Union were seen as the primary threat to US hegemony. The US Secretary of State George Marshall prepared a plan, better known as the Marshall Plan, for the "European Recovery Program". It called on the US Congress to allocate billions of dollars for the reconstruction of Europe. Japan was also rebuilt under the Marshall Plan. As part of the effort to rebuild global capitalism after the war, the US introduced the Benton Woods system of currency conversion and world trade. Under this system, the "gold standard" for conversion of foreign currencies of different countries and world trade was replaced by the US dollar. The US created bodies like the International Monetary Fund (IMF), World Bank and World Trade Organization (WTO) to control world economy and trade. The US wanted to manipulate the world economy so that it remained adapted inextricably to suit the US and European investors and their multinational companies. So the concept of globalization or free trade was introduced. The US does not believe in free trade for itself. It wants free trade only for non-western countries. Free trade has been imposed on the poor countries by the leaders of the US and the developed countries whose industries and commerce have been amply protected to ensure that the growth of US economy is assured. Under globalization most of the profits go to groups of American and European investors and their multinational corporations.

A large number of developing nations emerged as independent countries after the Second World War. Most of these countries were colonies of European nations like Britain, France, Germany, Spain, Portugal, Netherlands and Russia. Many countries of Asia, Africa and Latin America had waged struggles for independence from their foreign rulers and gained independence. At the time of independence they were impoverished and underdeveloped. Only the degree of impoverishment and underdevelopment differed. They were beset by poverty and illiteracy. They had no access to technology. Many of the regimes were totalitarian, elitist and corrupt. They were totally dependent on the developed nations for food, consumer products, funds and technologies required for development. Till the seventies, it often appeared that the developing countries would never develop. The situation is true for many of them even today.

Then came the Asian Tiger Economies like Singapore, South Korea, Thailand, Taiwan, Malaysia and Indonesia with a new "mantra" or concept of growth through foreign investments and exports to the developed countries. Fixed, government controlled conversion rates gave way to full convertibility and free market management. The developed countries poured in hundreds of billion dollars in direct investments and loans. Foreign companies set up manufacturing units in developing countries to take advantage of the cheap labour available there and exported the finished goods to their domestic markets and made huge profits. Spectacular growth rates of 8 to 10 per cent were sustained for decades. Share prices, real estate prices and per capita incomes grew at an enviable rate. For a while it seemed that at last an answer had been found to the problem of sluggish growth of developing nations. Then suddenly the bubble burst. In the face of collapse of the real state market, mounting foreign debt, shaky banks with large non-performing assets, flight of capital, raids by currency speculators and shrinking exports, hundreds of banks and businesses in the Asian countries went bankrupt. Millions lost their jobs. Currencies and stock markets crashed. Millions of dreams went sour. What went wrong?

The 21st century has seen the rapid rise of China and India on the world economic scene. China's growth has been truly spectacular and it has emerged as the world's third largest economy. India has also been able to sustain 8 to 10 per cent economic growth for more than 5 years. The spectacular GDP growth in both the countries has been made possible by large foreign investment and exports of goods and services to the developed world.

The world economy is again at crossroads today. The US and Britain are in recession. The growth in developed nations of Europe and America is stagnating. Some Asian economies have achieved remarkable growth in the past two decades as have Russia, Brazil, Argentina and Venezuela. But an US recession could severely affect some of these countries. Many middle income countries are stagnating. Sub Sahara African countries and a few countries in Asia like Nepal and Bangladesh continue to be in abject poverty.

Some economists have questioned the sustainability of the growth strategy of developing countries based on foreign investment and export-oriented growth. Developing markets are swamped with foreign consumer products. Stock markets in many emerging markets were booming on the back of investments from the developed world. All appears well. But is it actually so? Are we poised for sustained growth or are we also headed for collapse? IMF and World Bank have predicted a slowdown in the US economy. Some say it may be a short-term situation. Others feel that the weakness in US economy is more fundamental and could last for some time. The major question that we need to find an answer to is: How will a global economic slowdown affect the developing countries?

The World Economic Forum met in Davos, Switzerland in January 2008. Over 500 world leaders, businessmen, economists, and great corporate giants of the world attended the meeting. They agreed that 2008 is likely to see a slowdown in the US economy and consequently a slowdown in the world economy. They also agreed that 1.3 billion of the world's population (out of 6.2 billion) live on less than 1 or 2 US dollar per day. There was a consensus of opinion that globalization has left billions in abject poverty, and that it has increased the gap between the rich and the poor. The per capita income of the 10 richest nations of the world is 100 times that of the poorest 10. In 1960, they were only 30 times richer. However, the elite gathering could not agree on what to do about the situation except promising some debt relief and aid to the poorest nations of Africa.

The standard remedy for developing countries, insisted upon by the IMF, is to privatize, globalize, reduce government expenditure including subsidies, close down loss making banks and companies and control inflation. This means that the citizens of the country must endure a period of austerity to atone for the sins of their government. The Philippines has been doing just that for the last 40 years. But there is no prosperity in sight. Of the 89 countries following the IMF prescription since 1965, 32 have become poorer, 16 have stagnated. The wisdom and efficacy of the IMF formula for a turnaround is being questioned by many world economists including some at the World Bank.

Joseph Stiglitz of the World Bank puts it well: "Imagine that a country with a fixed exchange rate finds itself in a balance of payment crisis. It is importing too much and exporting too little (the exact situation that obtains in most developing countries). What can it do? It can impose some tariffs on imports but that is not allowed by the WTO. It can allow exchange rates to fall. It increases the cost of essential imports (like oil and technology in our case). It can impose austerity measures like higher taxes and cut public spending and thus kill the economy. Lack of money may reduce demands for imports but at what cost to economic growth?"

This book seeks to examine the validity of the neo-liberal capitalist concepts of privatization, globalization and export-oriented growth in the context of the developing world. It is a commonsense approach to development of economic policies for the developing world. In the process it hopes to dispel some myths like the wealth of the developed world is due to these capitalist policies called "Neo-liberal Capitalism" laid down by the Washington Consensus between IMF, the World Bank, the United States Treasury and their prodigy the WTO, that globalization is beneficial for poor nations, that export-oriented growth is the only path for economic development, that foreign aid and investment is essential and desirable for the prosperity of the developing nations. The book also seeks to suggest a different path to prosperity for developing nations. It is a middle path between the Neo-liberal Capitalism of the West and the "cradle to grave welfare" envisaged in communist and socialist countries. This is the concept of "Nationalism".

The concept of Nationalism is not new. Nationalism is simply doing what is in the best national interest. It is what Condoleezza Rice, US Secretary of State called "American Realism" during her address at the Economic Forum meet at Davos in January 2008. America and the other developed nations have been following this concept for years and have always acted in their own interests. America pays its farmers not to produce so that the prices of agriculture products do not crash. Europe is unwilling to abolish farm subsidies. The West does not need to practice Nationalism because the Neo-liberal Capitalism which they thrust on the developing world through the WTO serves their national interests to the full. But what about the developing nations? Will the IMF formula of privatization and globalization work for them? Or should developing countries follow the example of United States and Europe and act in their best national interest?

It is also appropriate at this stage to clarify a few aspects of the statistical data used in this book. There are various sources of economic data. For example, the PPP GDP of countries is compiled by World Bank, IMF, CIA World Fact Book, *The Economist*, etc. There is some difference in the figures given out by different sources. I would request the readers not to worry too much about the accuracy of the figures, which in any case, are constantly changing. It is the reality, enormity and trends behind the data quoted which hold a meaningful relevance to the views expressed in this book.

**Col. Bhaskar Sarkar**

# Contents

## PART II—**MODELS FOR DEVELOPMENT**



## PART III—**IMPLEMENTATION OF NATIONALISM**

# PART I

# DEVELOPING NATIONS AND THEIR PROBLEMS

# 1

# Wealth and Prosperity

## Wealth

The concept of wealth has changed over the period of time. In the age of the hunter gatherer, mankind did not have the concept of wealth. These forefathers lived from day-to-day, from moment to moment, risking their lives in the search of food for survival. It is a pity that while this has changed for most of the world population, there are many who still combat a different set of hazards to make both ends meet. Adults and children of many countries scrounge around in garbage dumps in search of saleable waste. Many sacrifice their health recycling hazardous chemical waste to earn a living. Others work in hazardous mines. Women are trafficked. Children and young men take up arms on behalf of war lords, terrorist organizations or political parties. Many grow or peddle drugs and take part in all kinds of criminal activities.

Once the primitive man settled down into homes, domesticated animals and began to grow food, wealth made its appearance. It was often measured by the number of heads of cattle or the number of wives. The practice is still prevalent among many primitive tribes. Then man discovered gold and precious stones. Slowly coins of gold, silver and bronze evolved and their possession along with gold, silver and precious stones signified wealth. The value of the coins was real in the sense that they represented the worth of the metal content of the coin. Slowly, the sizes of the dwellings, the number of servants or slaves were added to what construed wealth. Wealth was still real. It was tangible. It could not disappear by itself. People and nations fought for each other's wealth.

Then came paper money. It did not have any value of its own. It was a promise by the Government issuing it to pay on demand, the holder of the currency, the face value of the money in gold. For the first time money was unreal. It was not universally acceptable. It was valid only in the country of its origin. If it was to be used in a foreign land, it had to be converted into the other currency at a mutually agreed exchange rate which changes from time to time. In 1960, 100 rupees could buy about 13 dollars. Today it would be about two. In 1992, 1 US $ was equal to 144 Russian ruble. By 1996 it had become 1 US $ equal to about 6000 rubles. Money had ceased to reflect true wealth. The people of India are worried about the depreciating value of money. That is why they tend to convert their surplus money into gold or hard currency. The private holding of gold in India is estimated to be about 310,000 tons. 1200 tons of gold are imported every year into India to meet this craving for gold. It appears to be an unproductive practice. But who knows? In a few years, if the US dollar continues to be devalued at the current rate and price of gold continues to rise (it rose from $710 per oz in September 2007 to $934 per oz in January 2008), they may be considered wise. In spite of so many explanations like, the value of a currency reflects the economic fundamentals of the country, I do not really understand why it fluctuates as much as it does. Economic fundamentals do not change every day.

In the good old days wealth had to be physically removed. It had to be badly invested or be robbed or be looted to disappear. It could not disappear by itself. It is no longer so today. Today money in a safe can loose its value as you sleep if devaluation takes place or there is hyper inflation. If you do not believe it ask a Brazilian who was alive in the seventies or a Russian pensioner who visited garbage dumps in 1992 looking for food or a Korean factory worker or an Indonesian farmer after the Asian currency collapse of 1998 or a Zimbabwean of today.

Man was not satisfied with reducing wealth to paper currency. Gain or loss of wealth was too slow for the businessmen working on a fast track. Stock markets were established to trade and speculate in shares of companies. Value of shares was no longer restricted to the real value, i.e. the book value. Notional values based on future earnings, brand names, taxation policies, etc. entered the market. Gambling or speculation as it is called in the economic world, was permitted on a large scale, preferably with money that belonged to others, the unsuspecting gullible ordinary retail investors or obliging banks. Fortunes are now made or lost in moments. If you do not believe me ask those who invested in the shares like those of the US energy giant Enron on the US Stock market. If you do not want to go so far, ask the small investors who invested in Indian stock markets in 1992-93 or those who invested in the Indian stock markets and mutual funds during 2007-08. The lessons of the Wall Street crash of 1929 are mostly forgotten.

Man was not satisfied with simple form of gambling or speculation in the form of shares. They introduced trading in futures and derivatives or other obscure complicated financial instruments so that money could be made or lost faster than ever. The rules for this form of speculation are so complicated that even the so-called experts do not seem to understand them fully. If you do not believe me ask the investors of Barings Inc. or investment banks like Bear Sterns and Lehman Brothers of the US.

Then we have speculations in currencies. The big investors are buying and selling currencies to make profits. As a result, currencies of the various nations of the world are subject to large fluctuations. The currencies of the developing world are most vulnerable. But even the currencies of the developed world are not immune to the effects of this speculation. The yen was particularly volatile in the late nineties with 20 to 25 per cent changes in a matter of months. This makes long-term financial planning most difficult. The situation is serious enough for Germany to suggest fixing the limits of fluctuation between the three major currencies, the dollar, the Euro and the yen at the meeting of the G7 countries. The proposal was vetoed by the United States.

Wealth today is no longer tangible and solid. It is no longer based on the heads of cattle or number of wives or even number of cars or private aircraft. It is not based on your holding of gold and jewels. It is not based on the number or size of your mansions. It is based on your assets and your investments. You know what they are worth today. What will be their worth tomorrow? Your guess is as good as mine.

## Prosperity

Having seen the state of wealth of an individual, shall we try to find about his prosperity. Till about the nineteenth century the prosperity enjoyed by man was relatively simple and largely unchanged. He could have a palace of a house, a large retinue of servants, beautiful wives, concubines and horses. He could eat on a gold plate, entertain lavishly, patronize arts and crafts and have women fanning him to sleep on a hot day. There was a limit to prosperity. But then science changed it all. In came cars, television, airplanes, music systems, phones, mobile phones, hotels, holiday resorts, discos and night clubs, video and computer games, brand names and what have you. One can spend Rs. 50 million on a car or a few hundred thousand Rupees to buy a dress. You can become a space tourist for about $25 million. Suddenly, there is no limit to what you could have or do. The only limitations were your imagination and your physical ability. You needed Viagra to perform in bed. You needed drugs to keep away depression. You needed private banking to hide your wealth from your spouse and your creditors. But, in spite of all possible indulgences, a millionaire cannot spend all his money. This created a new problem. What to do with the surplus wealth. A few fools donated it in charity. But most reinvest their money to make more money. They devised more ingenious ways to speculate. Many invested in sub prime mortgage instruments. With the collapse of the housing market in the US, about a trillion dollars investment is at risk.

## Purchasing Power Parity

There is another aspect of wealth and prosperity which is difficult to understand. My son, a young software engineer working in Singapore earns about 4000 Singapore dollars or little over Rs. 100,000 per month. I, with thirty years of service, earn only about Rs. 40,000 as a senior engineer. He pays Rs. 35,000 for a two bedroom flat, whereas I would pay about Rs. 5000. He buys milk at Rs. 27 per litter, whereas I buy at Rs. 13. He pays Rs. 15 for a bus ticket. I would be paying Rs. 5 for a similar journey in Delhi. But a computer for him is just one week's salary whereas for me it is almost one month's salary. How do we compare wealth and prosperity. A baby sitter in the United States earns more in rupee terms per hour than I do. A poor family in Asia can be sustained for a month on the cost of a visit to the beauty parlor in the United States. Is such a comparison feasible or desirable? How can this be rationalized? And if this cannot be rationalized, how can there be globalization.

## Conclusion

There was a time when wealth and prosperity were real. The disparity between the rich and the poor was limited. Disparity in prosperity between nations was marginal. Things have changed. Over a billion of the earth's population live in unimaginable squalor in the developing countries on less than one US dollar per day. Over a million millionaires in the developed and developing countries do not know what to do with all their money. The GDP of many developing countries is less than the annual turnover of many multinational companies. Is the disparity between the "haves" and "have nots" here to stay and grow or can the developing countries find a way to improve the health, wealth and prosperity of their people?

# 2

# The Developed and the Developing World

## Classification of Nations

In India the people are divided into castes or classes. We have the "Brahmins" or the priests, the "Kshatriyas" or the warriors, the "Baishyas" or the businessmen or traders, the "Shudras" or the blue collared workers and the "Dalits" or out castes. The new world order for human beings is simpler. You have the rich, the poor and the middle class, which hangs in somewhere in-between the two.

There is also a classification of nations. The classification of a country is measured with statistical indexes such as national income, per capita GDP, life expectancy, the rate of literacy, etc. The UN has developed the Human Development Index (HDI), a compound indicator of the above statistics, to gage the level of human development for countries where data is available. Based on this method, countries can be classified as developing countries, developed countries and failed states.

A developing country is that country which has relatively low standard of living, an underdeveloped industrial base, a moderate to low Human Development Index (HDI) score, a moderate to low per capita income but which is in the process of economic development. In other words, all countries which are neither a developed country nor a failed state are classified as developing countries. There are three grades of developing countries:

*Newly Industrialized Countries or NICs*. They are nations with economies more advanced and developed than those in the developing world but not yet comparable with a developed country. NIC is a category between developed and developing countries, and it includes countries like South Africa, Argentina, Mexico, China, India, Brazil, Malaysia, Philippines, Thailand and Turkey.

*Emerging Markets.* These are countries with an economy that has been consistently developing over a longer period but without much progress in industrialization. They include Pakistan, Iran, much of South America, several of the Persian Gulf States, the countries of the former Warsaw Pact and others. Some also include NICs into this category.

*Poor Developing Countries.* These are developing countries with an inconsistent record of development. They include most countries in Africa, Central America, and the Caribbean (except Jamaica, in category 2, and Puerto Rico, much of the Arab World and also a few countries from Southeast Asia (Laos and Cambodia). Seventy-six per cent of the world's countries fall under this category.

Developed countries, in comparison, usually have economic systems based on continuous, self-sustaining economic growth and high standards of living.

Least developed countries or failed states are poor countries that have experienced prolonged periods of economic decline due to war, internal strife or bad governance. These countries could have suffered a long-term civil war or large-scale breakdown of rule of law or non-development-oriented dictatorship. Some examples are Afghanistan, Haiti, Somalia, Myanmar, Iraq, North Korea. These are not considered as developing countries for the purpose of this book.

There is another method of classification of countries. In this method the countries are divided into four categories, the First World, the Second World, the Third World and the Fourth World.

The term "First World Countries" refers to countries that are democracies, which are technologically advanced and whose citizens have a high standard of living. While there is no precise definition of the "first" or "rich" world, the World Bank does categorize countries as high, upper and lower middle, as well as low income. High income countries are thereby defined as countries with a per capita Gross National Income of US $11,116 or more. According to the World Bank, 60 countries were categorized as high income economies as of 2007. According to IMF, 31 countries are classified as "advanced economies". These countries are also called the Global North.

The Second World is a phrase that was used to describe the Communist states within the Soviet Union's sphere of influence. Many "Second World" countries are now considered part of the "First World". These countries include Russia, Poland, Hungary, the Czech Republic and some others.

The Third World is a term used to broadly categorize the developing nations of the world. These countries were mostly colonies of the European powers. They are also often referred to as the Global South.

The Fourth World or the Least Developed Countries are countries which according to the United Nations exhibit the lowest indicators of socio-economic development, with the lowest Human Development Index ratings. They meet the three criteria of per capita of less than US $750, human resource weakness on indicators of nutrition, health, education and adult literacy and economic vulnerability (based on instability of agricultural production, instability of exports of goods and services, economic importance of non-traditional activities, merchandise export concentration, and handicap of economic smallness, and the percentage of population displaced by natural disasters). The classification currently applies to around 49 countries (as of June 14, 2007).

## Disparity Between Nations

Let us see the economic statistics of the G7 Nations of the developed world:

| Nation | GDP in Billion $PPP | Population in million | Per Capita GDP, PPP | HDI | Growth Rate % |
|---|---|---|---|---|---|
| World | 72,337 | | | | |
| European Union | 14,935 | | | | |
| United States | 13,543 | 299 | 43,223 | .951 (12th) | 2.7 |
| Japan | 4,346 | 128 | 32,530 | .953 (8th) | 1.7 |
| Great Britain | 2,270 | 59 | 35,486 | .946 (16th) | 2.6 |
| France | 2,040 | 59 | 31,825 | .952 (10th) | 1.7 |
| Germany | 2,714 | 82 | 31,390 | .935 (22nd) | 2.6 |
| Italy | 1,888 | 56 | 31,051 | .941 (20th) | 0.7 |
| Canada | 1,217 | 32 | 35,514 | .961 (4th) | 2.7 |

It will be seen that the total combined GDP of the G7 countries is 28018 billion $ PPP. The populations of these countries add up to 715 million or about 12 per cent of the world population of 6.0 billion. The average per capita GDP works out to 39186 $ PPP. It is worth noting that though the per capita GDP is high, the growth rate is low compared to the developing countries.

Let us now see the economic statistics of the 10 most developed of the developing nations or Newly Industrialized countries:

| Nation | GDP in Billion $ PPP | Population in million | Per Capita GDP, PPP | HDI | Growth Rate % |
|---|---|---|---|---|---|
| China | 11,606 | 1314 | 8,832 | .770 (81st) | 10.1 |
| India | 4,726 | 1067 | 3,936 | .619 (128th) | 9.1 |
| Brazil | 1,717 | 186 | 9,193 | .800 (70th) | 2.7 |
| South Korea | 1,250 | 47 | 24,084 | .921 (26th) | 4.8 |
| Mexico | 1,249 | 102 | 11,369 | .829 (52nd) | 2.8 |
| Thailand | 645 | 64 | 9,193 | .781 (78th) | 5.6 |
| Taiwan | 749 | 23 | 30,687 | .925 (28th) | 4.6 |
| South Africa | 664 | 46 | 13,018 | .674 (121st) | 4.4 |
| Argentina | 643 | 39 | 16,512 | .869 (38th) | 4.6 |
| Malaysia | 342 | 24 | 11,374 | .811 (63rd) | 4.7 |

The total GDP of these 10 nations comes to 23,591 billion dollars PPP or about 80 per cent of that of the developed nations. The total population on the other hand comes to 3012 million or about 50 per cent of the world population. The per capita GDP works out to an average of 7,832 dollars PPP. The per capita

GDP is about one-fourth of that of the developed nations. But the growth rates are substantially higher.

Now let us see the situation in 10 of the poorest countries of the world:

| Nation | GDP in Billion $ PPP | Per Capita GDP, PPP | HDI | Growth Rate % |
|---|---|---|---|---|
| Nepal | 48 | 1947 | .534 (142) | 3.5 |
| Haiti | 16.5 | 1840 | .529 (145) | 3.5 |
| Ivory Coast | 32 | 1680 | .432 (166) | 1 |
| D R Congo | 54 | 842 | .411 (168) | 7.5 |
| Ethiopia | 95 | 1123 | .406 (169) | 8.9 |
| Kenya | 50 | 1357 | .521 (148) | 5.8 |
| Madagascar | 20 | 954 | .533 (143) | 4.5 |
| Malawi | 10 | 707 | .437 (164) | 8.5 |
| Tanzania | 33 | 806 | .467 (159) | 5.8 |
| Yemen | 22 | 984 | .508 (153) | 3.2 |

The GDP of these ten countries add up to 380 billion dollars PPP which is about one 700th of that of the GDP of the G7 nations. The per capita GDP is 1124 which is about one thirty-fifth of the average of the G7 countries. Mercifully, the rate of GDP growth is better than the G7 nations in most cases.

### Causes of Disparity Between Nations

The disparity between the developed and developing nations is there for all to see. It would be interesting to analyze the reasons for this disparity which are mainly historical, cultural and geographical.

*The first and little recognized reason for the disparity is recognition of "Human Rights".* The feudal systems followed in most nations were exploitive and encouraged exploitation of the working class and farmers by the priests and the hereditary ruling class. Literacy among the less privileged classes was discouraged as lack of education made exploitation easier. Serfs, slaves and other forms of bonded labor was common. The situation first changed with the proclamation of Magna Carta in England in 1215 which enshrined the human rights and constitutional rights of the common people and abolished serfdom and placed the ruler under the law of the land. The concept quickly spread to other parts of Europe and then to the United States. It led to the spread of education, improvements in the Human Development Index and growth in science and technologies in these countries. But the European powers and the American Pioneers did not grant human rights to the people of their colonies and to the native population of the lands they conquered and exploited. Thus, the Third and Fourth worlds were denied basic human rights till their countries gained independence. The concept of universal human rights was accepted only with the formation of the United Nation. Unfortunately, many Third and Fourth World nations have not granted full human rights to their own citizens by continuing to practice the feudal systems that perpetuate the position of the privileged. Lack of education and economic opportunities for the common people is a major factor which contributes to the disparity among nations. The blame for this state of affairs rests squarely on the developing nations themselves.

*The second most important reason for the disparity is industrialization.* Mechanization of farming and mass production of goods started in Britain in 1701. Mechanized weaving commenced in 1738 and the first spinning mill came up in 1764. The industrial revolution and tools of mass production spread to Europe and America. The sale of mass produced goods in their colonies, often at exorbitant and exploitive prices enriched Europe and America at the expense of the Third and Fourth World. The developed nations gained from the industrial revolution that took place in Europe. They have exploited the technological edge so gained to the hilt and got richer. The process still continues.

*The third reason is their colonial past.* Most of the developing nations of Asia, Africa and Latin America have been colonized for better part of three centuries or more by the developed nations. These colonies were systematically exploited by the developed nations. Their wealth has been taken away. Their mineral resources have been taken away. Little attention was given to the development of their infrastructure, particularly in the rural areas. Little attentions was paid to literacy and health care. Their industries were not allowed to develop. Their raw materials were taken away, value added and sold back at substantial profits. At the time of independence, the Third and Fourth World nations were left almost broke. In addition to colonization, there have been ethnic cleansing on a very large scale. In North America, parts of Central and Latin America, the ethnic Indian population was decimated and driven into reservations. Their gold and jewelry were usurped. Their lands were taken over without any compensation. In Australia the aborigines were almost wiped out. Then there was the use of slaves from Africa. These hapless people contributed to the prosperity of the Britain, European Countries like Spain and Portugal and United States by working on the farms and industries without compensation. Britain fought a war with China for the right to sell opium to the Chinese people and added insult to injury by taking Hong Kong as spoil of war.

*There were cultural reasons too*. The people of the developing world were mostly not ambitious and easy going. These countries neglected education and development of science and technology. Thus gun powder was discovered in China but converted to weapons in Europe. These weapons were used by the Europeans to conquer the world.

*There were geographical reasons too*. Most of the developing nations were blessed with abundant natural resources and warm climate. They did not have to forage outside the country for food or natural resources. Asia, Africa and South America were too far removed from Europe for the benefits of the industrial revolution to reach them. On the other hand, limited natural resources available in some of the developed nations, particularly in Europe and Japan were not adequate to sustain them. They conquered the world in search of mineral and other resources. The easy living and abundant availability of natural resources and a salubrious climate made the people of developing nations lazy, complacent, more accommodating and less aggressive. They were easy prey for the energy and aggressiveness of the developed world.

### Future of North-South Divide

History cannot be rolled back. The lead in technology of the developed world cannot be denied or easily overcome. Neither can their military superiority be denied. But the developed nations need the developing nations. If India and Australia were to refuse to export iron ore to Japan, the Japanese economy could well collapse. The Japanese would have to go to war again to ensure supply of such resources. Most of the crude oil used by the developed world comes from the developing world. The developed world also needs the markets in the developing world. With their small population, they just cannot consume what they produce. The construction companies of the developed countries cannot sustain themselves within their own countries. Their infrastructure is almost completed. Canada hardly needs to construct 100 km of roads per year. But the requirement of roads in the developing countries is in thousands of kilometers.

Globalization and opening up of the markets of the developing world is thus essential for the survival of the developed countries. Without liberalization, globalization and privatization, they are sunk. Their multinational corporations produce too much of goods and services and depend on globalization to find markets for their products. They do not have the raw material to stoke their industries. They depend on globalization to ensure supply of these raw materials. They have too much of investment funds. Funds, unless invested, do not produce returns. They need globalization and liberalization for optimum and profitable utilization of their surplus funds. Money is a powerful tool of domination. The developed world wants to dominate the developing world with their money.

Are the developed countries prepared to pay any price for cooperation from the developing world? Are they prepared to compensate the Third and Fourth World countries for the colonization and exploitation they have been subjected to for centuries? At the present they do not seem inclined to do so. They are not yet prepared to write off the debts of the poorest of the developing nations though the proposal has been put before the G7 nations a number of times. Only IMF loans to some of the poorest countries of Africa have been written off in 2007. At the moment the developed countries, particularly their multinational corporations, seem inclined to exploit their economic advantage to economically dominate and exploit the developing countries.

The developing countries need the developed countries. They need loans and investment for development. They need technologies to catch up with the developed world. They need the markets of the developed world to export their products and earn the foreign exchange to pay for imports of goods, services and technologies that they require to develop. What is the price they have to pay for cooperation and assistance from the developed world? If it is sovereignty, then I would consider the price too heavy to pay. At the moment it is economic sovereignty which they are required to pay.

Is there a middle ground for constructive engagement between the developed and the developing nations? Is there a way developing countries can obtain funds and technologies from the developed world without having to surrender their economic sovereignty? Is there a way of being able to get this assistance without being swamped by unrestricted imports from the developed world? Is there a way of getting the funds without being at the mercy of unrestricted inflow and outflow of funds that destabilizes the economies and currencies of the developing countries? Is there a way of carrying out trade and commerce without compromising on national interests? If we want a long term, mutually beneficial association we must find a way. The developing nations must have the right to choose what they want to import and when. They must get funds without conditions that impinge on their economic sovereignty. They must be able to manage their foreign exchange reserves and currencies in a way that serves the interest of the countries best. The economic arm twisting must stop. Forcible prizing open of markets must stop. Thrusting upon of western consumerism must stop. Destruction of domestic industries or their acquisition by multinationals must stop. Otherwise there will be confrontation instead of cooperation between the developed and developing countries. A few political leaders may be bought or persuaded to sign unequal treaties. A few scribes in the media can be bought to eulogize the benefits of free market reforms and globalization. But all people of a nation cannot be bought. The people of these nations have fought for independence from colonial rule. If necessary they will fight again to preserve or regain their economic sovereignty.

# 3

# Feasibility of Export Oriented Growth

The neo-liberal concept of economic liberalization, globalization and free trade can only work for the developing countries if they can export enough to earn the foreign exchange required to pay for the goods and services imported. Since the requirement is for hard currencies, the Dollar, the Euro or the Yen, the exports have to be mostly to the United States, Europe and Japan, crude oil exporting countries or other countries with large foreign exchange reserves like China, India, Taiwan, Singapore, Australia, etc. Can these countries import enough to sustain the industries in the developing world? Let us examine the possibility.

It is not out of place to mention that the exports from the developing world to the developed world is restricted to raw materials like crude oil, metal ores, coal and timber, grains, pulses, fruits and vegetables and agriculture based products jams, jellies, mushrooms, spices, marine products like shrimps and tuna, garments and handicrafts. Many of the products are processed and marketed by multinational corporations of the developed world.

## Exports to Developed Countries

Let us start with Japan, the third largest economy in the world. Japan has a population of about 125 million. It has a trade surplus of US $ 213 billion. But Japanese economy is in a poor state. In 2008, Ota Hiroko, the Minister of State for Economic and Fiscal Policy, announced that Japan's economy could no longer be considered 1st class economy due to a number of facts including the sixth straight annual decline in the country's per capita gross domestic product. The unemployment rate is 4.1 per cent. The figure is low by world standards but unthinkable in Japan a decade ago. Thirteen and half per cent of the population lives below the poverty line. The low birth rate and consequent negative growth in the population also effects growth. Fifty per cent Japanese are over the age of fifty, hardly the age to engage in consumerism. So it has little potential as a growing export destination for developing nations.

The situation in the European Union is more or less stagnant. There is no shortage of funds. Its unemployment rate is around 10.8 per cent of the work force, the highest in the developed world. The population growth rate is low. The IMF expects the Euro area economy to grow at about 2.4 per cent. However, the European Union gives preference to imports from the second world countries of Eastern Europe. Under the circumstances, a 2.4 per cent growth can hardly sustain a 4 per cent or more growth in exports from the developing world.

The United States is the biggest economy in the world. It has a population of about 300 million. The rate of unemployment is about six per cent, at its highest in recent years. The US economy is in deep trouble. After reporting robust growth of about 4 per cent till the third quarter of 2007, the growth dropped to 0.06 per cent in the fourth quarter. The housing and real estate bubble has burst with housing prices falling in real terms for the first time since the Great Depression. The Sub-Prime mortgage business has collapsed as a result. This in turn has sucked out liquidity from the banks and financial institutions of US and Europe. Many international banking giants like Citigroup, Merryl Lynch, UBS, Paribas, Credit Swisse, Norther Rock have made stunning losses in the fourth quarter of 2007. The US dollar had to record lows against the Euro, British Pound and some other currencies like the Indian Rupee. Gold had climbed to over 900 US $ per oz on the back of weakening US dollar and lack of investor confidence in the stock markets. Crude oil prices touched 140 US $ per barrel before dropping below 60 US $. The Fed has been repeatedly cutting interest rates and pumping in hundreds of billion dollars of emergency liquidity into the financial sector in a desperate attempt to improve investor confidence and stock markets. President Bush has introduced a 150 billion $ economic package to improve consumerism. But no one seems to be sure that recession in the US can be staved off. It will be obvious that given the state of US economy, exports to the US will decline rather than increase in the near future, if ever.

Canada is a developed nation and a G7 country. It has a population of just about 30 million. However, in view of its small population, it cannot be considered to be a major export destination for the developing world.

It would be clear from above that the possibility of the developing world growing at a rate of 4 to 6 per cent through exports to the developed world is remote. In fact the trend could be exactly the opposite. The developed world would seek to export more to the developing world to sustain their economies and prevent a collapse.

## Exports to Oil Exporting Countries

Oil producing countries have plenty of foreign reserves and hence are possible export destinations. Let us see the economic vital statistics of some of the major oil producing countries:

| Nation | Population millions | Per Capita GDP PPP | Foreign Exchange Reserve | Foreign Debt Billion $ US | Current A/c Balance Billion $ US |
|---|---|---|---|---|---|
| Russia | 141 | 12178 | 484 | 287 | +68 |
| Indonesia | 217 | 4356 | 57 | 130 | +10 |
| Nigeria | 151 | 1227 | 54 | 6 | +14.6 |
| Iran | 66 | 8535 | 71 | 15 | +19 |
| Saudi Arabia | 23 | 16505 | 32 | 47 | +89 |
| Kuwait | 2 | 20886 | 20 | 20 | +51 |
| UAE | 3 | 34109 | 25 | 39 | +36 |

Crude oil prices had touched record levels after rising steadily on the back of rising demand from developing countries like India and China. The economies of the oil producing nations are booming. But the possibility of significant growth in exports to these countries from the developing nations except to Russia and Iran is almost non-existing because of their small population and consumer base.

## Exports To Newly Industrialized Countries

This category of developing nations with their excellent growth rates, large population base and growing foreign exchange reserves are perhaps the future growth engines of the world economy.

| Nation | Population millions | Per Capita GDP PPP | Foreign Exchange Reserve | Foreign Debt Billion $ US | Current A/c Balance Billion $ US |
|---|---|---|---|---|---|
| China | 1319 | 7722 | 1695 | 305 | +336 |
| India | 1067 | 3936 | 288 | 132 | –18 |
| Brazil | 180 | 9193 | 187 | 177 | +10 |
| Argentina | 37 | 16513 | 46 | 106 | +7.4 |
| South Africa | 46 | 13018 | 32 | 55 | –16 |
| South Korea | 47 | 24084 | 261 | 229 | +3.7 |
| Thailand | 62 | 9193 | 115 | 57 | +8.6 |
| Malaysia | 24 | 16512 | 101 | 57 | +25 |
| Mexico | 101 | 11364 | 79 | 178 | –5.4 |

It will be seen from the above figures that these countries, particularly China and India with their vast population and large foreign exchange reserves could act as export destinations for developing countries. With rapid industrialization, these countries have a large demand for raw materials and energy. Their rapidly expanding middle class has enormous appetite for consumer goods. Even the developed nations are eyeing these markets.

## Export Earnings

Export earnings depend on the price of commodities. Let us see the price situation for some of the commodities over the last 12 years:

**Commodity Price in US $ (World Bank Figures)**

| Commodity | Jan 2007 | Jan 2006 | Jan 2005 | Jan 2004 | Jan 2003 | Jan 2000 | Jan 1995 |
|---|---|---|---|---|---|---|---|
| Rice (Tonne) | 320 | 300 | 250 | 200 | 200 | 245 | 310 |
| Wheat (Tonne) | 210 | 160 | 150 | 160 | 150 | 100 | 200 |
| Sugar (Tonne) | 240 | 380 | 180 | 140 | 170 | 120 | 250 |
| Coffee (Kg) | 2.8 | 2.8 | 2.8 | 2.9 | 1.4 | 2.5 | 3.0 |
| Tea (Kg) | 1.8 | 2.0 | 1.8 | 1.55 | 1.5 | 1.9 | 1.5 |

*(Contd.)*

| | | | | | | | |
|---|---|---|---|---|---|---|---|
| Rubber (Kg) | 2.4 | 1.8 | 1.2 | 1.2 | 0.9 | 0.6 | 1.5 |
| Cotton (Kg) | 1.25 | 1.25 | 1.25 | 1.6 | 1.25 | 1.1 | 2.0 |
| Gold (Troy oz) | 650 | 550 | 450 | 400 | 350 | 260 | 390 |
| Aluminum (Tonne) | 2800 | 2300 | 1800 | 1600 | 1300 | 1700 | 1800 |
| Crude Oil (Barrel) | 90 | 65 | 50 | 30 | 30 | 28 | 20 |
| Soy Beans (Tonne) | 300 | 250 | 250 | 250 | 350 | 210 | 280 |
| Maize (Tonne) | 160 | 160 | 95 | 115 | 110 | 95 | 120 |

It would be seen that most commodity prices of agricultural products, metals, energy and food produced and exported by the developing countries have been rising since 2007 after a few years of record lows but still have not reached the figures of 1995 in some cases. The export earnings of most of the developing countries are therefore rising. But it has to be seen whether the volumes can be sustained in the face of the slowing down of economies of the US and some of the developing countries.

Export oriented growth in the developing countries can only be sustained if the demand for their products rise in the developed world and its price. Demand for any product, whether within the world or within a country is finite at a given period of time. If the supply exceeds demand, goods and services will remain unsold. Prices will fall. Bottom lines of the manufacturers will fall. Some will make losses.

The supporters of free market will argue that the fittest will survive and there is nothing to be concerned about. But many like me will disagree. Survival of the fittest is the law of the jungle. It is not the law of the modern society. In modern society every one must survive and live with dignity. When a company becomes bankrupt, too many people are hurt. The workers lose their jobs. The investors lose their money. The banks who lent money to the company are left with large bad debts. If the bank had too much exposure to the company, it could also be in trouble. The banks become wary of giving loans and try to become over selective in giving loans. This makes it difficult for new companies to raise money. Mindless competition is not in the interest of the society. Humanity and cooperation is. In any case, the multinationals, with their larger size and greater staying power have a better chance of surviving competition than the smaller domestic industries of the developing world. Developed countries with large tax incomes can and do subsidize.

their agricultural products to ward off competition from the developing world making it even more difficult for developing countries to export their products. Then the developed countries are experts at raising non tariff barriers like use of child labor, unfair labor practices and apprehensions about quality to stop imports of products of the developing countries and protect domestic industries. If uncontrolled competition is permitted, all the domestic industries of the developing world will have to close down. That is certainly not in the best interest of the developing countries.

Demand can rise if there is appreciable growth in population and if the poor get richer and have more money to spend. Neither of the conditions is met in the developed world. The population growth in these countries is either stagnant or growing at a rate of 1 per cent or less. With relocation of manufacturing to developing countries like China, India and Vietnam and large scale out sourcing of information technology, financial and health services, the unemployment is increasing. The capitalist system followed by the countries also ensures that the rich get richer and the poor get poorer. Thus there are 38 million Americans living below their poverty line and one million is being added to this number. The conditions required for export oriented growth does not exist. In spite of all the hard sell by the IMF and the WTO, developing countries can never grow through exports to the developed world. The worst is that they cannot even earn enough dollars to import food, energy and technology that they desperately need.

Since the possibility of exports to the developed world is stagnating and may well reduce in the near future, the only option left to the developing countries is to increase trade amongst themselves and to exploit their domestic markets. The biggest hurdle here is the requirement of foreign exchange for international trade. Most of the poor developing countries require food, consumables and consumer durables, petroleum products, cars and commercial vehicles. To import these items, the countries need foreign exchange. Most countries do not export enough to earn the foreign exchange required to finance the imports. Hence they have to depend on foreign investment, foreign aid or foreign loans to get the required foreign exchange. To get foreign investments or loans, they have to create an environment to generate so called "Investor Confidence". This investor confidence is achieved only if the economic sovereignty of the country is surrendered to the IMF. Laws have to be passed to permit free flow of investment, funds, goods and services in favor of the developed countries. Laws have to be passed to permit foreign acquisition of land, properties and companies. In the long run this could lead to acquisition of all prime land, properties and businesses by foreign nationals. This would ultimately lead to the loss of political sovereignty as well.

## Other Options

Is there a way to prevent this calamity? Fortunately, there is. These are barter trade, balanced trade and local currency trade.

Barter trade has been known from time immemorial. It involves the exchange of commodities between nations at a mutually agreed rate. This type of trade has been initiated by Malaysia with great success. Under this system, Malaysia imports rice from Pakistan and exports Palmoline oil in return. This type of trade requires no foreign exchange and hence can be successfully conducted by even the poorest countries.

Balanced trade implies that the exports and imports between two countries be more or less equal in US dollar terms. Thus very little foreign exchange is required for a very large volume of trade. The concept has been elaborated upon in the Chapter "Foreign Exchange Management and the Developing World".

The local currency trade is also in existence. All trade between the Soviet Union and India has been in Rupees till 1991. This enabled India to import military hardware, crude oil and technology from Russia without having to pay in scarce foreign exchange. Tea, garments, consumer durables were bought by Russia with the Rupees so earned. The United States also sold grains to India in the sixties on a similar basis under the PL 480 scheme. Under this scheme, India paid for its food grain imports from United States in Rupees. The United States used these rupees within India for welfare projects as foreign aid. In local currency trade, the country purchases its imports with its own currency at a mutually agreed exchange rate between the currencies of the importing and the exporting countries. This could be based on the price of gold in local currencies of the two countries. The local currency earned by the exporting country is used to meet the cost of setting up marketing and after sales servicing costs, the cost of running embassies or high commissions, tourism and travel to these countries, setting up business ventures in the country. Local currency trade has the following benefits for developing countries:

- It eliminates the requirement of foreign exchange for imports and thus increases volumes of trade. Even the poorest countries will find it easier to import their necessities.
- It cuts out competition from the developed world and their multinational companies.
- This form of trade will reduce availability of surplus stocks in the exporting countries and help in boosting prices of goods and services and bottom lines of companies in the developing countries.
- The increases in trade will boost industries, generate employment and pull the developing countries out of industrial slowdown.
- It reduces outflow of foreign exchange and reduce dependence on foreign investment and foreign exchange loans.
- It will increase the overall prosperity in the developing nations.

## Conclusion

The vision of export oriented growth is a mirage. It is a goal the hungry developing nations can never reach in the long run. They can never export enough to earn foreign exchange required to meet the requirements of unrestricted imports of goods and services from developed nations as visualized in the

WTO agreement. The demand in the developed world is just not enough to absorb all the exports of the developing world.

The consequences of failing to earn enough foreign exchange to pay for the imports are going to be disastrous. Foreign exchange loans will increase till the debt trap is closed. There will be default on loans. The local currencies will be substantially devalued. The local cost of essential imports like oil, food grains and technologies will sky rocket. The domestic industries will collapse one by one. There will be hyper inflation like what we have seen in Brazil, Russia and Indonesia. Unemployment and poverty will rise. The countries will be run by the multinationals through proxy as we see happening in some of the smaller Latin American countries. The poor will be driven to crime. There will be social unrest. Life and property will not be safe.

Even the developed nations will not escape the catastrophe. As the economies of the developing nations collapse one by one, exports of the developed nations to these countries will fall. The profits of the multinationals will fall. There will be mergers and down sizing. Unemployment will rise. The economies of the developed nations will suffer.

There is only one way the world as a whole can prosper. Let us not think only of profits. Let us not persevere with greed as our religion. Let us not look for short-term growth. Let us seek slower and sustainable growth. Let us try to evolve a world system where one country does not have to grow at the cost of others but a system whereby all countries of the world can grow together. Let us evolve a system that takes care of the interest of all nations and not only that of the developed few. Do we have leaders who can see the certain failure of export oriented growth? It is unlikely. They are either too busy surviving the present to look into the future or have been bought by the multinationals of the developed world or their domestic associates.

# 4

# IMF and the Developing World

## Origin and Policies of IMF

The International Monetary Fund was conceived in July 1944, when the representatives of 45 governments met in the town of Benton Woods in New Hampshire, United States of America, and agreed on a framework for international economic cooperation. It is one of the Benton Woods Institutions devised by the US to ensure its economic hegemony in the world. The IMF was formally established in 1945, when the first 29 countries signed its Articles of Agreement. The International Monetary Fund or IMF was established in to finance reconstruction of the countries devastated by the Second World War. Once its primary role was over, IMF became a tool in the hands of the US and developed countries to usurp the economic sovereignty of developing nations.

The key to foreign trade is foreign exchange or the Dollar, the Yen or the Euro. The developing countries generally import more than they can export. They also need funds for development and import of technologies. They borrow money from the World Bank and foreign banks or financial institutions from time to time to meet their requirements of development and imports. The domestic companies of the developing countries, their foreign collaborators and the subsidiaries of the multinationals also indulge in private borrowing of foreign exchange and imports. Foreign investors in the country's stock exchanges also repatriate their profits or withdraw their investments. Thus, the foreign exchange reserves of many of the developing countries are low and decreasing. Periodically they have a balance of payment problem. In other words, they do not have enough foreign exchange to meet their debt repayment obligations. This creates a crisis situation in the country and amongst its lenders. This is when IMF steps in. It provides foreign exchange to developing nations in need of foreign exchange to meet balance of payment requirements by giving low interest dollar loans. Between 1965 and 1995, IMF has lent money to 89 countries, both developing and the developed. On the face of it, the purpose appears very noble. But in reality it is like an old fashioned village money-lender or landlord lending money to a poor farmer to marry off his marriageable daughter. But there appears to be a hidden agenda. These loans serve two very useful purposes for the developed countries. These are:

- It ensures that the investment made by the developed nations in the form of loans by its banks and investments by its multinationals and financial institutions like mutual funds and pension funds are safe. If these funds are not provided and the country is unable to pay their dues, it is these institutions of the developed world which would suffer along with those of the developing countries. It ensures that the developing country has enough foreign currency to carry on importing goods and services from the developed world.
- It forces the governments of the developing countries to adopt certain economic policies which are not always in their best interests, particularly for their poorer sections of the society and which they would not otherwise adopt. In other words the IMF usurps the economic sovereignty of the country.

IMF financial aid is always bound by certain conditions including Structural Adjustment Programs. These conditions, which are the economic performance targets established as a precondition for IMF loans, often retard social stability and lead to an increase in poverty in recipient countries. The IMF also recommends currency devaluation to the governments of poor nations with struggling economies. Such policies are destructive to economic prosperity. The IMF sometimes advocates "austerity programs", increasing taxes even when the economy is weak, in order to generate government revenue and balance budget deficits, which is the opposite of Keynesian policy. These policies were criticised by Joseph E. Stiglitz, former chief economist and Senior Vice President at the World Bank, in his book *Globalization and Its Discontents*.

Current IMF rules prohibit members from linking their currencies to gold.

IMF policy makers have always supported military dictatorships which were friendly to American and European corporations. The IMF is generally apathetic or hostile to their views of democracy, human rights, and labor rights. Some of the tyrant regimes supported by IMF are listed below. The list is by no means exhaustive.

| Country | Dictator | Period | | Debt in Billion $ | | |
|---|---|---|---|---|---|---|
| | | From | To | At start | At end | Net |
| Argentina | Military | 1976 | 1983 | 9.3 | 48.9 | 39.6 |
| Bolivia | Military | 1962 | 1980 | 0 | 2.7 | 2.7 |
| Brazil | Military | 1964 | 1984 | 5.1 | 105.1 | 100 |
| Chile | Pinochet | 1977 | 1991 | 5.2 | 18 | 12.8 |
| El Salvador | Military | 1979 | 1994 | 0.9 | 2.2 | 1.3 |
| Indonesia | Suharto | 1967 | 1998 | 3 | 129 | 126 |
| Kenya | Moi | 1979 | 2002 | 2.7 | 6.9 | 4.2 |
| Pakistan | Zia-ul-Haq | 1977 | 1988 | 7.6 | 17 | 9.4 |
| Pakistan | Military | 1990 | 2008 | 20.6 | 29.9 | 9.3 |
| Philippine | Marcos | 1965 | 1986 | 1.5 | 28.3 | 26.8 |

All figures in Billion US Dollars.

## Conditions of IMF Loans

The IMF financing never comes without conditions which are generally never made public. These include Structural Adjustment Programs which are the economic performance targets established as a precondition for IMF loans, retard social stability and lead to an increase in poverty in recipient countries. Currency devaluation is recommended by the IMF to the governments of poor nations with struggling economies. The IMF also advocates "austerity programs", increasing taxes even when the economy is weak, in order to generate government revenue and balance budget deficits. The country must reduce government subsidies, even if such subsidies are beneficial to the poorer sections of the society or the domestic industries. The IMF is unconcerned if the food prices treble and the people of the country are made to suffer tremendous hardships. They, however, have no objection to Europe subsidizing its farm products or United States paying its farmers for not cultivating and creating a government department to eradicate mountain lions and wild sheep to benefit its cattle farmers. The country must privatize its public sector industries and services, preferably to foreign companies and multinationals. This also creates job-losses and benefits the multinationals who get an entry into the core sectors of the country. The country must reform its banking system by closing down banks with large non-performing assets and loss making mutual funds. The IMF is unconcerned by the losses the investing public in the developing countries are likely to suffer as a result of these measures. It is, however, not averse to re-capitalizing of Japanese, US or European banks with taxpayers' money. It is also not averse to bailing out of the hedge fund, Long Term Capital Management, in the United States when it made over a billion dollar loss while trading in futures and derivatives. The country must close down its loss making companies even if such measure result in sky rocketing unemployment and spells doom for its shareholders and financing banks. The core belief of the IMF is that a developing country can only prosper through inflow of foreign investment and export oriented growth. IMF insists that the country must create so-called investor confidence by enabling free movement of foreign capital into and out of the country. The other measures recommended to build this confidence are a convertible currency, enactment of laws enabling foreign acquisition of land and properties and better laws for recovery of debt. These policies were criticized by Joseph E. Stiglitz, former chief economist and Senior Vice President at the World Bank, in his book *Globalization and Its Discontents*.

## Failures of the IMF Prescription

The IMF success record is dubious. Its prescription for the developing countries and recipients of its loans is not infallible. Between 1965 and 1995, 89 nations were placed under IMF care. Economies of 16 of these countries have stagnated. Thirty-two of these countries have become poorer. That means the IMF prescription has not worked in more than 50 per cent of the cases.

Since 1980, over 100 countries or most of the Fund's membership have experienced a banking collapse and reduction of GDP by four per cent or more. Jamaica is one of the countries which followed the IMF's policies and suffered. In 1978, one year after Jamaica first borrowed money from the IMF, the Jamaican dollar was worth more than the US dollar on the open exchange. By 1995, when Jamaica stopped following IMF policies, the Jamaican dollar had eroded to less than 2 cents US.

Argentina, experienced a catastrophic economic crisis in 2001 which were caused by IMF-induced budget restrictions. The restrictions undercut the government's ability to sustain national infrastructure even in crucial areas such as health, education and security, and led to privatization of strategically vital national resources to the benefit of multinational corporations. The crisis led to widespread hatred of IMF in Argentina and other South American countries, with many blaming the IMF for the region's economic problems.

Another example of where IMF Structural Adjustment Programs aggravated the problem was in Kenya. Before the IMF got involved in the country, the Kenyan central bank oversaw all currency movements in and out of the country. The IMF mandated that the Kenyan central bank had to allow easier currency movement. However, the adjustment brought in very little foreign investment, but allowed some businessmen to siphon off billions of Kenyan shillings in what came to be known as the Goldenberg scandal, leaving the country worse off than it was before the IMF reforms were implemented.

IMF intervention is always accompanied by increase in unemployment and poverty. In Indonesia the percentage of population in poverty increased from 11.3 per cent to about 20 per cent. In South Korea it increased from 15.7 per cent to about 23 per cent. In Thailand it increased from 15.1 per cent to about 22 per cent. The IMF style market reforms never benefit the poorer sections of the society. In Vietnam it meant that the country grew plenty of food but its citizens were woefully under fed. Vietnam exported 3.5 million tons of rice in 1997. Yet 42 per cent of its children and 45 per cent of the women population were under nourished. Seventy-five per cent of the children suffered from anemia. The IMF market reforms are responsible for not sharing the fruits of increased production with its farmers.

### *Reasons for Failure*

It is perhaps necessary to examine why the IMF prescription of Structural Reforms have failed. One issue is foreign exchange reserves and the ability of a country to earn enough foreign exchange to pay for its imports and meet its foreign debt payment obligations. This is the obligation of the government of a country. But the governments are not solely responsible for its foreign exchange debts. It is true that the governments do borrow money from IMF and the World Bank. But in a free market economy, the domestic companies and local subsidiaries of the multinational corporations are also free to import and arrange finance for their activities through foreign exchange borrowings from foreign banks and financial institutions. In Indonesia, the private foreign debt was over 40 per cent of the total foreign debt of the country. The free market reforms insist that the government should not interfere with the working of the private companies and multinational corporations. Thus, the government has no control over private borrowings. So how can the government be responsible for the private foreign debt of the domestic companies and subsidiaries of the multinationals? The governments are not responsible to ensure that loans provided by domestic banks to the same companies are repaid. So why should they ensure that the industry repays the loans provided by foreign banks. The decision to give the loans was based on normal commercial considerations of profit and greed. Why should the governments be responsible for these decisions and be held liable.

The governments of countries forced to usher in free market reforms by the IMF have another major problem in managing their foreign exchange reserves. In the free market environment, they have no control over imports. The developed countries are keen to export as much as they can. The result is that a lot of non essentials like consumer goods, consumer durables, cigarettes and liquor are imported. As exports cannot keep pace with imports, there is a trade deficit and shortage of foreign exchange. A balance of payment problem brings in its wake currency devaluation resulting in costlier imports of essential commodities like oil and food and a host of other problems.

Let us see the foreign exchange management of countries who had taken IMF loans:

| Nation | Imports | Exports | Trade Deficit | Current A/c Balance | Foreign Exchange Res. | Foreign Debt |
|---|---|---|---|---|---|---|
| Argentina | 31 | 46 | None | +7.4 | 46 | 106 |
| Bolivia | 1.8 | 2.4 | None | +1.3 | 3.9 | 5.9 |
| Brazil | 91 | 137 | None | +10 | 187 | 177 |
| Chile | 36 | 59 | None | +8.2 | 18 | 48 |
| El Salvador | 4.1 | 2.5 | 1.6 | –9.3 | 2 | 8.8 |
| Indonesia | 40 | 63 | None | +10 | 56 | 130 |
| Kenya | 3.2 | 2.2 | 1 | –1 | 2.6 | 6.6 |
| Pakistan | 31 | 20 | 11 | –6.5 | 15 | 42 |
| Vietnam | 22 | 20 | 2 | –1.2 | 20 | 22 |
| Philippine | 54 | 43 | 11 | +9 | 34 | 61 |

All figures in Billion US $

It will be seen from the above figures that most countries who have accepted loans from IMF except Brazil and Vietnam have foreign debts far in Excess of their foreign exchange reserves. The governments of developing countries must be allowed a free hand to manage their foreign exchange reserves and trade balances. They can do this successfully only if they have full control over borrowing of foreign exchange and imports by their domestic companies and the subsidiaries of foreign multinationals operating in their country. They must also have full control over imports of goods and services and a right to choose what is to be imported and when. This freedom is denied to the governments of the developing countries who take IMF loans because the free market reforms, which are an essential condition of grant of these loans, do not permit exercise of control over imports and private foreign exchange borrowings. It is perhaps for this reason that Malaysia opted to face the South East Asian meltdown in 1998 without recourse to IMF aid. They were unwilling to surrender their economic sovereignty. There may have been a slow down in the growth of their economy. But they have managed to retain sound economic fundamentals. Their foreign debt to foreign reserves ratio is very healthy as compared to some of the other developing nations who have borrowed from IMF. The following figures will bear that out.

| Nation | Foreign Debt Billion $ US | Foreign Exchange Reserve Billion $ US | Ratio |
|---|---|---|---|
| Malaysia | 57 | 101 | 1:1.77 |
| Indonesia | 130 | 57 | 1:0.44 |
| Argentina | 106 | 46 | 1:0.43 |
| Pakistan | 42 | 15 | 1:0.36 |
| Philippines | 62 | 34 | 1:0.55 |
| Chile | 47 | 18 | 1:0.38 |
| Kenya | 6.6 | 2.6 | 1:0.39 |

China has not borrowed money from IMF. Neither does it follow the IMF dictates of free market reforms. It has opened up its markets in a controlled manner on a strictly reciprocal basis. It has kept its national interests in the forefront of its policy making. So has Malaysia. They practice their own brand of economic nationalism.

## Conclusion

The developing countries cannot survive with profit as its god and greed as its religion. Neither can the developed nations. If the wealth and prosperity of the world is to be ensured, then the "nation" must be the god and "prudence" must be the sustaining religion. Growth should be slow but sustainable. Funds should be used with prudence where required to generate income and not to create surpluses of goods and services leading to deflation, bankruptcies and collapses. Countries must have the freedom to regulate inflow and outflow of funds so that funds are invested where required and not to generate over capacities. The countries must have the freedom to regulate imports and private debt so that foreign exchange reserves can be successfully managed and there are no payment crisis.

There is one positive which needs to be mentioned. In 2005, the IMF was the first multilateral financial institution to implement a sweeping debt-relief program for the world's poorest countries known as the Multilateral Debt Relief Initiative. By year-end 2006, 23 countries mostly in sub-Saharan Africa and Central America had received total relief of debts owed the IMF.

If the aim of the establishment of the IMF was to meet the foreign exchange requirements of the developing world, it has been a resounding success. If the aim of establishing it was to bring wealth and prosperity to the countries it finances, it has failed more often than it has succeeded. In many cases, 32 out of 89, its free market reforms have actually made the countries poorer. Its policies are designed to protect the interests of the developed nations and not those of the developing nations.

# 5

# WTO and the Developing World

## Concept and Role of WTO

The World Trade Organization or WTO came into being on January 1, 1995 and replaced the General Agreement on Trade and Tariff or GATT as the forum for world trade policy and a dispute settling body. The World Trade Organization deals with the rules of trade between nations at a near-global level. It is responsible for negotiating and implementing new trade agreements, and is in-charge of policing member countries' adherence to all the WTO agreements, signed by the bulk of the world's trading nations and ratified in their parliaments. Most of the WTO's current work comes from the 1986-94 negotiations called the Uruguay Round, and earlier negotiations under the GATT. The organization is currently the host to new negotiations, under the Doha Development Agenda launched in 2001. The WTO's headquarters are in Geneva, Switzerland.

The WTO has 151 members (almost all of the 123 nations participating in the Uruguay Round signed on at its foundation, and the rest had to get membership). On January 11, 2007, Vietnam became the 150th WTO member state. Tonga finalized ratification of the admittance in July 2007, and thus became the 151st member state.

A number of non-members have been observers (32) at the WTO and are currently negotiating their membership: Algeria, Andorra, Azerbaijan, Bahamas, Belarus, Bhutan, Bosnia and Herzegovina, Cape Verde, Comoros, Equatorial Guinea,

Ethiopia, Holy See, Iran, Iraq, Kazakhstan, Laos, Lebanon, Libya, Montenegro, Russia, Samoa, Sao Tome and Principe, Serbia, Seychelles, Sudan, Tajikistan, Ukraine, Uzbekistan, Vanuatu and Yemen. Observers must start accession negotiations within five years of becoming observers. Syria's application is pending since 2001. The fourteen states and territories so far have no official interaction with the WTO: the states of Eritrea, Somalia, Liberia, Turkmenistan, North Korea, Monaco, San Marino, East Timor, Nauru, Tuvalu, Palau, Kiribati, Micronesia, Marshall Islands and the territories of Western Sahara, Palestine.

The entire concept of WTO is based on promoting unrestricted trade across the globe. A creation of the Washington consensus of the IMF, World Bank and the United States treasury, it created the vision or perhaps illusion that free and unrestricted trade will benefit all nations and bring prosperity to all. The basic tenants of the WTO are as under:

- All member countries will permit unrestricted imports of goods, industrial or agriculture based, and later services like banking, insurance, securities, shipping, telecommunication and information technology.
- The countries will reduce import duties progressively over a period of time to almost zero levels. They will not be permitted to increase import duties to reduce imports.
- Countries will not be permitted to use subsidies to protect domestic industries and agriculture.
- Intellectual property rights as defined in the rules of WTO will be protected by the member countries who will pass appropriate laws within a laid down timeframe in their countries to ensure that the aims are achieved.
- Free movement of capital and investment across borders will be permitted by member countries.
- All trade related disputes between the member countries related to the observation of WTO rules will be adjudicated by the WTO whose decision will be final and binding on the countries.

### WTO is Unfair to Developing Nations

The rules appear to be fair to all. But unfortunately it is not so, particularly for the developing world. The entire system is loaded in favor of the developed world. As we have seen in the chapter, "The Developed and the Developing World", the developed countries enjoy considerable advantage in technology and financial resources. WTO allows the developed countries and particularly their multinational companies to exploit this advantage. It is the developed countries which have gained the most from WTO. In this connection it is relevant to quote from an article written by Sir Leon Brittan, European Commissioner, in an article titled "Everybody free up please" in the "World in 1998", brought out by the magazine *Economist.* It says "Europe needs to remember how much it has gained from the WTO. The EU has scored a major success, for example, in opening the whiskey market in Japan, where taxes have fallen by 44 per cent. It has used WTO to limit discriminatory taxation against imports of (European) cars into America and it is defending the interest of the European car industry in Indonesia and Brazil. In many cases the mere existence of WTO has acted as an effective deterrent, preventing action which would otherwise be seriously damaging to Europe's commercial interests." It is a frank and revealing statement. What he has uncharitably forgotten to mention is that the WTO has served the European and American commercial interest by opening up the markets of the developing world to Kellogg's corn-flakes, Coca Cola, McDonald hamburgers, Kentucky fried chicken, Pizza Hut pizzas, various types of scotch whiskeys, cigarettes, shirts, T-shirts, jeans, cars, consumer durables and a host of other things: It is obviously irrelevant that in the process the trade deficit of developing countries has increased by a few billion dollars. It is that many additional billions dollars gain to the economies of the developed countries.

WTO is a one way street where a developing nation opens up its market without any reciprocity from the developed nations. Exports from developing countries are still subject to the same old restrictions. Its garment exports are still restricted by quotas. Its stainless steel exports have been subjected to anti-dumping duties. Its exports of canned mushrooms have been subjected to additional duties. Its marine industries are banned for not using turtle proof nets. Its carpets are banned for use of child labor. Its export of technical manpower in the software industry is sought to be curtailed by insisting that they be paid the same wages in America as an American citizen. Japan does not permit import of rice or full opening up its market. Europe and the US continue to subsidies their farm and dairy products.

WTO is a system of the developed nations, devised by the developed nations for the developed nations. Its sole aim is to prize open the markets of the developing world to the products and multinational companies of the developed world. This has been done to compensate the developed countries for the lack of growth in their own domestic markets by enabling them to export their surpluses to the developing world. And the system is working exactly as it was intended to.

The industries of the developing countries are not in a position to compete with foreign multinationals. The industries of the developing nations lack the technology and financial clout of the multinationals. They cannot survive price wars with the multinationals. It is an unfair competition. You do not have juniors competing with seniors in any sports event. The industries of the developing nations are juniors in trade and commerce. They must get the handicap to make it a fair competition.

Developing nations with their large foreign debts, poor export earnings, adverse trade balance and tenuous foreign exchange reserves cannot afford unrestricted imports. Unless restriction of trade is permitted they are going to be swamped by foreign debt.

WTO is the result of unequal treaties between the developed and the developing nations. The so-called entry negotiations were dominated by economic arm twisting and short-term inducements. Any right minded developing nation must get out of the WTO as early as possible.

Martin Khor, Director of the Third World Network, argues that the WTO does not manage the global economy impartially, but in its operation has a systematic bias toward rich countries and multinational corporations, harming smaller countries which have less negotiation power. He argues that developing countries have not benefited from the WTO Agreements of the Uruguay Round, because (among other reasons): market access in industry has not improved; these countries have had no gains yet from the phasing out of textiles quotas; non-tariff barriers such as anti-dumping measures have increased; and domestic support and export subsidies for agricultural products in the rich countries remain high. The Third World Network has called the WTO "the most non-transparent of international organizations", because "the vast majority of developing countries have very little real say in the WTO system".

## Benefits of Getting Out of WTO

The developing nations will do well to get out of the WTO as early as possible. This will provide them many benefits. It will enable them to stop the import of non-essentials and thus conserve precious foreign exchange. It will enable them to tax imports and generate much needed revenue. Since most of the imported consumer goods are premium products intended for the premium market segment of the dirty rich, who have unlimited capacity to pay, this is not going to hurt anyone but will help to fund infrastructure and social justice. It will be able to use taxation of imports and subsidies for protection of domestic industries and agriculture. Reduction of imports will take the pressure off from exports. It will no longer be necessary to export at all cost. The developing countries will, therefore, be able to hold on to commodities for longer periods and obtain better prices for their exports of agricultural products and raw materials to the developed countries.

Introduction of barter trade and local currency trade will lead to enlargement of the markets in the developing world and quicker disposal of surplus production within the developing countries. This will reduce pressure to export and ensure more remunerative prices. For example, if Malaysia could not export a few million tons of Palmoline oil to Pakistan through barter trade, the surplus so generated would have pushed down the prices of Palmoline oil and hurt the manufacturers in Malaysia.

Another example is the surplus electric power available in Pakistan. India needs the power but may not be able to afford the foreign exchange drain. If the power could be bartered with other imports from India, both countries would benefit. It will enable the developing countries to develop technologies without paying royalties for intellectual property rights. The Indian pharmaceutical industry has benefited from this practice for years. India, against its interest, is seeking to change its sovereign Patent Act to benefit the US and EU. China has benefited from the same in its electronic industry. The developed countries have exploited and colonized the developing countries for centuries. What is wrong if the developing countries catch up with western technologies without paying for it?

The developed countries will try their level best to stop the developing countries from getting out of WTO. There will be threats and inducements to remain within the fold. There will be economic sanctions. There will be economic arm twisting of every type. Some will succumb. But the brave will benefit. There may be some short-term difficulties. But in the end the requirements of profit and greed will prevail. The developed countries cannot survive without the markets of the developing world. They need the natural resources from the developed world. After India carried out its nuclear tests in May 1998, Japan imposed sanctions and cut off development aid. But it did not stop importing iron ore from India. It did not stop Japanese companies from entering the Indian market with their products.

## Conclusion

Most of the developing countries are poor negotiators. At best they lack in self-confidence and holding power. At the worst their political leaders are influenced by inducements. All developing countries can survive without imports of foreign products or foreign investment in stock markets. We Indians are used to living without uninterrupted electricity and water supply. We are used to walking, to cycle rickshaws, bullock carts and camel carts. Ninety-five per cent of the population of our country does not use any foreign consumer goods. We have lived under these conditions for hundreds of years of colonial rule of the same developed nations. We can do so for a few years more if required to preserve our economic sovereignty. Most of the population of the developing countries has nothing to loose. Unfortunately, the negotiators (political leaders), the rich and the powerful have.

WTO does not serve the interest of the developing world. Unless the conditions of membership are drastically changed to ensure economic sovereignty of the developing nations, it is in the best interest of the developing nations to pull out as early as possible and get into bilateral and multilateral trade agreements. Forty-six countries of the world including countries like Russia, Iran, Syria, Algeria, Belarus, Lebanon, etc. are not members of WTO. Thirty-two of these countries have applied for membership but have not accepted the terms of agreement offered. Most of these countries are economically sound with trade surpluses, robust foreign exchange reserves and high to middle Human Development Index. So why is it necessary to surrender economic sovereignty to the US and EU through the WTO.

# 6

# Foreign Investment and the Developing Countries

## Necessity and Types of Foreign Investment

IMF believes that developing nations cannot survive without foreign investment. The view is also shared by most of the bureaucrats, economists and industrialists of the developing nations. To an extent this is correct. Developing countries need investment in developing infrastructure and industries. The remarkable growth rates achieved by the Asian Tiger economies of the 1990s and China and India are largely due to the billions of dollars of investment that came into these countries in infrastructure, real estate and manufacturing. But these investments were not made with the aim of helping these countries. Some of the investment in infrastructure came from financial institutions like the World Bank and Asian Development Bank. But the major investments in real state and manufacturing were made by private investors or multinational corporations in search of profits which they cannot earn in the developed countries.

Foreign investments are in essence of two types:

- Foreign investments in the stock markets of the developing countries.
- Foreign investment in setting up manufacturing or marketing facilities through establishment of subsidiaries of multinationals or in collaboration with the domestic industries.

### Foreign Investment in Stock Markets

Foreign investments in the stock markets are fairly liquid funds. The foreign financial institutions can sell their holdings at any time and take away the money. Hence this kind of foreign investment is known as "Hot Money". Today's technology allows flow of billions of dollars from one country to another at the press of a button. The outflow of hot money reduces the foreign exchange reserves of the developing country. If the outflow is large it effects the foreign exchange conversion rate. In the free market system, the value of a currency is determined by its demand and supply. Outflow of "hot money" generates a large demand for foreign currency in a short period of time and at the same time reduces supply. If the liquid foreign exchange reserves of the developing country are low, outflow of hot money can lead to devaluation of the local currency of the developing country. Points out Mr. Jagdish Bhagwati of Colombia University, "In 1996, the total private capital inflows to Indonesia, Malaysia, South Korea, Thailand and the Philippines were 93 billion US $, up from 41 billion US $ in 1994. In 1997 that inflow suddenly changed to an outflow of 12 billion US $." This small outflow was enough to trigger the collapse of South East Asian economies in 1997, a collapse from which these countries and the world are yet to recover. "The claim of enormous benefits from free capital mobility", wrote Bhagwati, "are not persuasive". Mr. Paul Krugman, of the Massachusetts Institute of Technology, similarly concluded that the instability caused by huge capital movements required some policy response. Options range from taxes to discourage short-term capital outflow, like those employed by Chile and Malaysia or rules prohibiting such outflows. These measures are seen as unwarranted by some of the economic experts of the West. Most of the investors are banks and financial institutions like hedge funds and pension funds of the developed countries. Naturally the United States and the IMF are skeptical and against such controls. The dangers from existence of hot money in the economies of the developing countries are there for all to see.

Foreign investments in the stock market of developing countries tend to create other problems. Such investments create a situation of too much money chasing too few shares. The share prices get a boost, not due to any improvement in the fundamentals of the scrip's or performance of the companies, but simply because of availability of the additional funds in the market. This results in a bubble. Local fund managers are happy because they make some quick money. But in the long run, when the funds move out due to any reasons whatsoever the bubble bursts. The share prices crash. This hurts a lot of investors and results in a loss of investor confidence. The South Korean composite index fell by about 50 per cent between 7/97 and 9/98. The Thai Stock Exchange crashed by over 66 per cent in the same period. The Jakarta composite index also fell by more than 50 per cent in the same period. 17 Billion US $ were invested by foreign investors in the India stock exchange in 2007. It pushed the Bombay Stock Exchange Index (BSE Index) from about 10000 points to 21000 points. In January 2008, the foreign investors withdrew about 4 billion US $ from the market resulting in a 4000 point fall in the index. Many small investors, mutual funds and speculators have been badly hurt. Another large sell off by foreign investors in the wake of the current banking crisis in the west caused by US Sub-prime investment losses have caused a crash of the India Stock Markets and resulted in turmoil in the banks and financial services in India.

There is another effect of short-term foreign investment in the stock market that needs to be considered. The funds are invested to make profits. These profits have to be repatriated in foreign exchange every year to pay dividends to the investors. This generates an outflow of foreign exchange which is over and above imports. This makes it imperative on the governments of the developing nation to earn more foreign exchange in real terms than what is required to meet the cost of unrestricted imports. That is quite impossible as we have seen in Chapter 3, 'Feasibility of Export Oriented Growth'.

Short-term foreign investments in the stock exchanges of the developing countries are, at best, a mixed blessing. At the worst, it can result in a national economic disaster.

## Direct Foreign Investment

Direct foreign investments in creation of infrastructure or establishing manufacturing or marketing facilities are not as dangerous as short-term foreign investment in the stock market or "hot money". But uncontrolled direct foreign investment can also create problems. Between 1992 and 1996, more than 100 billion US $ were directly invested in the Asian Tiger economies. A large part of the funds went into creation of real-estate and setting up of factories or shipyards. Unrealistic ambition and availability of easy money led to unrealistic projection of demands. Over capacities were created in all industries. There were no buyers for the surplus real-estate. Real-estate prices crashed in Malaysia, Thailand, South Korea and the other Asian Tigers. Unfinished sky scrapers dotted the skyline of Jakarta, the capital of Indonesia when the author visited the country in 1999. The Hyundai shipyard in Korea does not have enough ships to build. There is over capacity in production of cars, consumer durables, electronics and almost every other items. Sales and bottom line of many companies dropped. The companies were unable to pay back the investors. The boom days saw a huge increase in employment and per capita earnings. This led to uncontrolled spending and imports. Once the downturn started, it snowballed into an international economic crisis where everyone has been hurt. There is deflation and recession. The unemployment is rising. Dreams have been shattered. It took the Asian Tigers about 10 years to get out of the mess created by the meltdown of 1998. Another threat looms in the horizon in the form of US recession in 2008.

The foreign investors invest in a developing country to make profits. They choose the sector in which they want to invest. Naturally they want to invest in low gestation, low investment, high return areas like cosmetics, food industries, automobile industries, consumer durables, liquor and cigarettes. Thus, over capacities are created. There is unhealthy competition. Some companies are bound to perish, bringing in misery to the investors and employees.

There is also the foreign exchange problem. In small developing countries, the multinationals set up export oriented units to take advantage of the cheaper labor costs and favorable exchange rates and export to the developed world. This is beneficial to the developing nation as there is increase in exports. But in large countries like India, China, Indonesia, the local market is what the foreign investors want to exploit. This is not always beneficial to the developing country as this harms the domestic industries and can create over capacities. The goods and services produced by the multinationals are sold in the local currency but profits are repatriated in dollars. This results in an additional drain on foreign exchange reserves of the developing country and puts pressure on the currency.

The foreign investors are generally reluctant to invest in the infrastructure like roads and power generation. The investment and gestation periods are large. The returns are slow in coming and recoveries are uncertain in the absence of efficient tariff collection systems. These projects can also result in serious foreign exchange problems. The sales are in local currencies but the return on investment and import of equipment have to be paid for in dollars. The developing countries find it difficult to earn enough dollars to make the foreign exchange payments.

Most of the leaders, economists and media persons tend to ignore the foreign exchange management problems associated with foreign investment. Some believe that further foreign exchange investments will generate the foreign exchange for repatriation of profits. Some are interested only in their short-term political or economic gains and somehow solving the current problems created by low foreign exchange reserves. Others simply believe that they would not be around when the problems begin to manifest themselves and the opposition party would have to face the crisis situation. The theory that additional direct investment will take care of the foreign exchange requirements of repatriation of profit does not work in the long run. It has not worked for the economies of the Asian Tigers. It is not going to work in the long run for the economies of the developing countries.

## Conclusion

Bank or private loans do not enrich individuals or companies unless the money so obtained can be invested to generate enough money to repay the loans and still retain some profits. In the case of nations accepting foreign exchange, the problem is still worse. The investments must not only generate adequate returns in the local currency, they must also generate adequate returns in foreign currency to permit remittance of profits. This is easier said than done. The problem is more acute in large developing countries like India and China whose markets are considered to be the killing fields by the developed countries.

Foreign investments in developing countries should only be acceptable if the investment leads to exports and generation of foreign exchange for repatriation of profit. However, such conditions are not acceptable to Japanese companies operating in India. Japan is referring the problem to WTO. It would be interesting to see what happens.

Developing countries must do their best to grow without foreign investment in their stock exchanges and consumer industries. This will slow down the growth. But it may be better to have a slow but sustainable growth than to achieve a fast growth and then crash.

# 7

# Multinationals and the Developing World

## Multinational Companies

Multinational companies are large corporations of the industrialized world engaged in almost every form of economic activity including manufacturing, agricultural production and marketing, providing service industries like banking, insurance, hospitality, health care, education, information technology and so on all around the globe. These companies contribute billions of dollars in tax revenue to their respective governments and generate employment in the countries where they operate. Their financial clout makes them very powerful. Some of the readers will be surprised to know that out of world's 100 largest economies, 51 are global corporations. That means that the sales of a large number of transnational corporations exceed the GDP of many Third World countries of the world. The list of these 100 largest economies is attached at the end of this chapter.

It is really interesting to see what American President Thomas Jefferson had to say about American corporations who over the years have grown in gigantic proportions.

> "I hope we shall...crush in its birth the aristocracy of our moneyed corporations, which dare already to challenge our government to a trial of strength and to bid defiance to the laws of their country."
>
> —Thomas Jefferson, in a letter to George Logan. November 12, 1816.

Not only have the US and most of the world failed to fulfill the hopes of the farsighted President, who foresaw the tyranny and power of the transnational corporates over two hundred years ago, we are allowing them to take control of our governments and our live. A large percentage of our leaders and government employees are on their covert pay rolls or accept funds for their election campaign or as bribes and do their biddings as corporate employees. Power and sophistication of the media produces evermore powerful ways of influencing how people think and what they believe. Big business distorts our perception of the truth. Corporate propaganda and some times even money power also tries to undermine democracy by supporting right wing leaders and conspiring to overthrow left leaning leaders. The purpose is to control the public mind. Because the big business realize that that the public mind is the greatest hazard facing them and that democracy is its real threat to private tyranny just as it is a threat to state tyranny. The fact that democracy is a threat to private business helps to explain the extraordinary scale of the efforts made to indoctrinate the people with the capitalist story. If you are interested to know more about the crimes that transnational corporations commit or powers they wield, you may like to visit the internet site www.corporations.org. Multinational Corporations are a major threat to the developing countries and their governments. Because of their financial clout, these companies are in a position to influence their own and the local governments.

## Multinational Companies and Regime Change

At the end of the Second World War, the US emerged as the largest economic power of the world. The multinational corporations contributed to its economic power. With the establishment of the United Nation, colonization became out of fashion. The only option available to the United States and its allies to achieve their objective of global domination was economic colonization. The multinational corporations became useful allies in this quest. They provided valuable sources for intelligence agencies like the CIA. They could and were used for canalizing funds for subverting assertive elected governments, purchasing political influence, organizing demonstrations, insurgencies, coups and bringing about regime changes. Some examples are given below:

Crude Oil was the source of nearly all Iran's national wealth. Muhammad Mossadeq became prime minister of Iran in April 1951. The Anglo Iranian Oil Company was nationalized. This was resented by the US and Britain. A coup was planned and assisted by CIA and British Intelligence to regain their control over Iranian oil. The Iranian Army overthrew the government of Mossadeq. A new government was formed with the deposed Shah of Iran back in the throne in September 1951. Mossadeq was convicted of treason in December and executed. Iran became affiliated with the Western military alliance through the Baghdad Pact in 1955, later the Central Treaty Organization. Muhammad Mossadeq was ousted because he dared to act in the interest of his people and his country and dared to act against the economic interests of Britain and the US and their transnational corporations.

Colonel Jacobo Arbenz Guzman, a hero of the 1944 revolution that brought democracy to Guatemala, was elected president in 1951 with the largest majority in Guatemalan history. But his attempts to strengthen national independence, the take over unused land belonging to US transnationals and the inclusion of communists in his government aroused the ire of the US State Department and Central Intelligence Agency. Guzman was overthrown.

Patrice Lumumba became the first and only elected Prime Minister of Congo in June 1960. Belgian companies controlled mining copper, gold and uranium in Congo. The Belgian government became worried that the companies could be nationalized. They engineered revolt in the mineral rich province of Katanga. Lumumba was delivered into the hands of his enemy, President Tschombe of Katanga and killed. Thus Patrice Lumumba, the first and only elected prime minister of Congo, was hunted and killed by Belgium and the US. He was hunted by the Belgiums who killed him because he was a nationalist, anti Belgium (the colonial rulers) and had worked against the economic interest of Belgium and its mining corporations. The

US tried to kill him because he appeared to be getting close to Soviet Union. Fortunately for them, the Belgians got him first.

Allende was elected President of Chile in the election of 1970. He was an ardent Marxist and an outspoken critic of capitalism. The US had substantial economic interests in Chile through large multinational corporations which could potentially be nationalized or expropriated by a socialist government. During Nixon's presidency, U.S. officials attempted to prevent Allende's election by financing political parties aligned with his enemy Jorge Alessandri. US transnational corporation ITT gave at least $350,000 to Jorge Alessandri. The CIA was confident in Alessandri's victory, and did not see the need to fund Alessandri directly. Allende assumed presidency on November 3, 1970. After his inauguration, Allende began to carry out his platform of implementing sweeping socialist programs in Chile. This included nationalization of large-scale industries (notably copper mining and banking), a thorough reform of the health care system, a reform of the educational system, a program of free milk for children. Allende also intended to improve the socio-economic welfare of Chile's poorest citizens. October 1972 saw the first of what were to be a wave of confrontational strikes. A CIA report released in 2000 admitted that the CIA financed this trucker's strike. Allende's increasingly bold socialist policies combined with his close contacts with Cuba, heightened fears in Washington. On September 11, 1973 the Chilean military, led by General Pinochet, at the behest of CIA staged a coup against Allende. Salvador Allende was killed because he was a socialist and a nationalist and his economic policies were not in the interest of US transnational corporations. He is neither the first nor the lasts. The strikes, coup and other attempts to remove the Venezuelan President, Hugo Chavez are almost identical to what happened to Allende.

## Degradation of Environment

A number of multinational corporations like Olam International Limited are involved in deforestation and illegal timber trade in the equatorial rain forests of developing countries like Congo, Brazil and Indonesia. World Banks private lending arm, International Finance Corporation Ltd. has held equity in Olam. World Bank assisted Olam in getting logging rights. Multinational Corporations like Cargill are clearing rain forests in the Amazon basin of Brazil and growing soya which is converted to chicken feed. Coca Cola has been accused of allowing effluents from its plants in India to pollute rivers and groundwater.

## Double Standards

Multinationals like Mosanto and Bayer are selling genetically modified seeds and agricultural products like wheat, rice, cotton, etc. which are not permitted in the developed countries. According to the Canadian Wheat Board, 87 per cent of Canadian wheat buyers now require non-genetically engineered certification of wheat. But some developing countries like Peru, Sri Lanka, Pakistan and Yemen are willing to accept genetically engineered wheat. In 2000 a scandal involving a gene, which was used to create Star Link GE corn, cost the US agro-biotech industry US $1 billion. Sony, Ericsson, Samsung and Nokia use toxic chemicals in many of their products and toys, particularly in their exports to the Third World. Multinationals like Bayer and Dow Chemicals regularly sell carcinogenic pesticides banned in developed countries in Third World.

## Patenting Indigenous Products, Medicines

Some multinational corporations have tried to patent traditional indigenous products of the developing countries. For example one tried to patent "Basmati Rice" which has been a traditional produce of India and Pakistan. Others have tried to patent traditional medicinal products from trees and herbs which have been in use in developing countries for thousands of years. Preventing such actions requires constant monitoring and costly litigation in the Patent courts of the US and EU.

## Incetives

Multinationals have played an important role in economic development of developing countries. Countries and sometimes different regions of countries have to compete against one another for the establishment of MNC facilities that generate tax revenue, employment, and economic activity. To compete, countries and regional political districts offer incentives to Multinational Corporations such as tax breaks, pledges of governmental assistance or improved infrastructure or lax environmental and labor standards. This process of becoming more attractive to foreign investment can be characterized as a race to disaster, a push towards greater freedom for corporate bodies, or both.

## Arm Twisting

Because of their size, multinationals can have a significant impact on government policy, primarily through the threat of withdrawing from the market. For example, in an effort to reduce health care costs, some countries have tried to force pharmaceutical companies to license their patented drugs to local competitors for a very low fee, thereby lowering the price. When faced with that threat, multinational pharmaceutical firms have simply withdrawn from the market leading to limited availability of advanced drugs. In these cases, governments have been forced to back down from their efforts. When companies are faced with the option of losing a core competitive technological advantage and withdrawing from a national market, they may choose the latter. This withdrawal often causes governments to change policy. Countries that have been most successful in this type of confrontation with multinational corporations are large countries such as India and Brazil, which have viable indigenous market competitors.

## Lobbying

Multinational corporate lobbying is directed at a range of business concerns, from tariff structures to environmental regulations. There is no unified multinational perspective on any of these issues. Companies that have invested heavily in pollution control mechanisms may lobby for very tough environmental standards in an effort to force non-compliant competitors into a weaker position. For every tariff category that one multinational wants to have reduced, there is another multinational that wants the tariff raised.

## Conclusion

Multinational corporations if properly regulated can be very useful in the economic progress of the developing countries. Post financial liberation era in China and India has experienced a huge influx of multinational companies in India and China. They have propelled the economy of the countries to greater heights. Majority of these companies are of American origin. But in recent years, more and more firms from European Union like Britain, Italy, France, Germany, Netherlands, Finland, Belgium, etc. have outsourced their work to India. Finnish mobile handset manufacturing giant Nokia has the second largest base in India. British Petroleum and Vodafone represent the British. A host of automobile companies like Fiat, Ford Motors, Piaggio, etc. from Italy have opened shop in India with R&D wing attached. French Heavy Engineering major Alstom and Pharma major Sanofi Aventis are some of the earliest entrant in the scene and are expanding very fast. South Korean electronics giants Samsung and LG Electronics and small and mid-segment car major Hyundai Motors are doing excellent business and using India as a hub for global delivery. Japan is also not far behind with host of electronics and automobiles shops. Companies like Singtel of Singapore and Malaysian giant Salem Group are showing huge interest for investment in India.

There is a need for governments of developing countries to control the corporate behavior of multinational corporations. The threat of nationalization (forcing a company to sell its local assets to the government or to other local nationals) or changes in local business laws and regulations can limit a multinational companies power as has been seen in Venezuela. The developing countries must remain vigilant about undesirable activities of multinationals like selling hazardous chemicals or pesticides banned in the developed countries, selling genetically engineered seeds and foodstuff without government approval, patenting traditional products and polluting the environment. The countries should also exchange information about nefarious activities of multinational corporations and act in unison against them when such action becomes necessary.

**Table Showing 100 Largest Economic Entities of the World**

| Rank | Country | Corporation | GDP (US $ mil) | Sales (US $ mil) |
|---|---|---|---|---|
| 1 | United States | | 8,708,870.00 | |
| 2 | Japan | | 4,395,083.00 | |
| 3 | Germany | | 2,081,202.00 | |
| 4 | France | | 1,410,262.00 | |
| 5 | United Kingdom | | 1,373,612.00 | |
| 6 | Italy | | 1,149,958.00 | |
| 7 | China | | 1,149,814.00 | |
| 8 | Brazil | | 760,345.00 | |
| 9 | Canada | | 612,049.00 | |
| 10 | Spain | | 562,245.00 | |
| 11 | Mexico | | 474,951.00 | |
| 12 | India | | 459,765.00 | |
| 13 | Korea, Republic | | 406,940.00 | |
| 14 | Australia | | 389,691.00 | |
| 15 | Netherlands | | 384,766.00 | |
| 16 | Russian Federation | | 375,345.00 | |
| 17 | Argentina | | 281,942.00 | |
| 18 | Switzerland | | 260,299.00 | |
| 19 | Belgium | | 245,706.00 | |
| 20 | Sweden | | 226,388.00 | |
| 21 | Austria | | 208,949.00 | |
| 22 | Turkey | | 188,374.00 | |
| 23 | | *General Motors* | | 176,558.00 |
| 24 | Denmark | | 174,363.00 | |
| 25 | | *Wal-Mart* | | 166,809.00 |
| 26 | | *Exxon Mobil* | | 163,881.00 |
| 27 | | *Ford Motor* | | 162,558.00 |
| 28 | | *DaimlerChrysler* | | 159,985.70 |
| 29 | Poland | | 154,146.00 | |
| 30 | Norway | | 145,449.00 | |
| 31 | Indonesia | | 140,964.00 | |
| 32 | South Africa | | 131,127.00 | |
| 33 | Saudi Arabia | | 128,892.00 | |

*(Contd.)*

| Rank | Country | Corporation | GDP ( US $ mil) | Sales ( US $ mil) |
|---|---|---|---|---|
| 34 | Finland | | 126,130.00 | |
| 35 | Greece | | 123,934.00 | |
| 36 | Thailand | | 123,887.00 | |
| 37 | | *Mitsui* | | 118,555.20 |
| 38 | | *Mitsubishi* | | 117,765.60 |
| 39 | | *Toyota Motor* | | 115,670.90 |
| 40 | | *General Electric* | | 111,630.00 |
| 41 | | *Itochu* | | 109,068.90 |
| 42 | Portugal | | 107,716.00 | |
| 43 | | *Royal Dutch/Shell* | | 105,366.00 |
| 44 | Venezuela | | 103,918.00 | |
| 45 | Iran, Islamic Rep. | | 101,073.00 | |
| 46 | Israel | | 99,068.00 | |
| 47 | | *Sumitomo* | | 95,701.60 |
| 48 | | *Nippon Tel & Tel* | | 93,591.70 |
| 49 | Egypt | | 92,413.00 | |
| 50 | | *Marubeni* | | 91,807.40 |
| 51 | Colombia | | 88,596.00 | |
| 52 | | *AXA* | | 87,645.70 |
| 53 | | *IBM* | | 87,548.00 |
| 54 | Singapore | | 84,945.00 | |
| 55 | Ireland | | 84,861.00 | |
| 56 | | *BP Amoco* | | 83,556.00 |
| 57 | | *Citigroup* | | 82,005.00 |
| 58 | | *Volkswagen* | | 80,072.70 |
| 59 | | *Nippon Life Insurance* | | 78,515.10 |
| 60 | Philippines | | 75,350.00 | |
| 61 | | *Siemens* | | 75,337.00 |
| 62 | | Malaysia | | 74,634.00 |
| 63 | | *Allianz* | | 74,178.20 |
| 64 | | *Hitachi* | | 71,858.50 |
| 65 | Chile | | 71,092 | |
| 66 | | *Matsushita Electric Ind.* | | 65,555.60 |
| 67 | | *Nissho Iwai* | | 65,393.20 |
| 68 | | *ING Group* | | 62,492.40 |
| 69 | | *AT&T* | | 62,391.00 |
| 70 | | *Philip Morris* | | 61,751.00 |

*(Contd.)*

| Rank | Country | Corporation | GDP ( US $ mil) | Sales ( US $ mil) |
|---|---|---|---|---|
| 71 | | *Sony* | | 60,052.70 |
| 72 | Pakistan | | 59,880.00 | |
| 73 | | *Deutsche Bank* | | 58,585.10 |
| 74 | | *Boeing* | | 57,993.00 |
| 75 | Peru | | 57,318.00 | |
| 76 | Czech Republic | | 56,379.00 | |
| 77 | | *Dai-Ichi Mutual Life Ins.* | | 55,104.70 |
| 78 | | *Honda Motor* | | 54,773.50 |
| 79 | | *Assicurazioni Generali* | | 53,723.20 |
| 80 | | *Nissan Motor* | | 53,679.90 |
| 81 | New Zealand | | 53,622.00 | |
| 82 | | *E. On* | | 52,227.70 |
| 83 | | *Toshiba* | | 51,634.90 |
| 84 | | *Bank of America* | | 51,392.00 |
| 85 | | *Fiat* | | 51,331.70 |
| 86 | | *Nestle* | | 49,694.10 |
| 87 | | *SBC Communications* | | 49,489.00 |
| 88 | | *Credit Suisse* | | 49,362.00 |
| 89 | Hungary | | 48,355.00 | |
| 90 | | *Hewlett-Packard* | | 48,253.00 |
| 91 | | *Fujitsu* | | 47,195.90 |
| 92 | Algeria | | 47,015.00 | |
| 93 | | *Metro* | | 46,663.60 |
| 94 | | *Sumitomo Life Insur.* | | 46,445.10 |
| 95 | Bangladesh | | 45779.00 | |
| 96 | | *Tokyo Electric Power* | | 45,727.70 |
| 97 | | *Kroger* | | 45,351.60 |
| 98 | | *Total Fina Elf* | | 44,990.30 |
| 99 | | *NEC* | | 44,828.00 |
| 100 | | *State Farm Insurance* | | 44,637.20 |

*Sources*: Sales: Fortune, July 31, 2000. GDP: World Bank, World Development Report 2000.

# 8

# Inflation and the Developing World

## Necessity and Benefits of Inflation

One of the conditions imposed by IMF on developing countries is that the government must control inflation. To achieve this, the countries are supposed to reduce government spending and privatize. Is this control of inflation beneficial to the developing countries? Will it help the developing countries catch up with the developed countries in terms of per capita GDP? Let us examine the issue.

As per the report of the Director General ILO (1980), the sectarian break up of employed people of the world are as under:

| Sectors | Developed Countries | Developing Countries |
|---|---|---|
| Agriculture | 12.65% | 65.15% |
| Industry | 36.70% | 14.95% |
| Services | 50.65% | 19.70% |

In India, the agricultural population is more than the average for developing countries. As per Planning Commission report, it was about 74 per cent of the total population in 1991. The per capita GDP of the rural population was about Rs. 2997 or roughly 70 US $. The per capita GDP of the urban population was about Rs. 10,844 or about 250 US $ for the same period. The per capita GDP of the urban population is therefore more than 3.5 times that of the rural population. The disparity is increasing. It was less than 3 times in 1981 and less than 2 times in 1951. If this disparity is to reduce, the rural GDP has to grow. In urban areas salaries keep increasing every year. The dearness allowance of government employees and the employees of the organized sector keeps increasing. But there are no such increases in the rural sector. How will the GDP of the rural areas grow? The area under cultivation cannot increase as almost all cultivable land is under cultivation. Improved irrigation, hybrid seed and better farming techniques can increase production. But increased production does not necessarily imply increased earnings. In the absence of adequate marketing facilities and export of surplus production, increased production generally means lower prices. Thus onions which were selling at Rs. 20 to 60 per kilogram in 1998 are selling at Rs. 8 to 10 per kilogram in 2007. Potatoes which were selling around Rs. 12 per kilogram in 1998 are selling at Rs. 8 to 10 per kilogram. Farmers are also vulnerable to unfavorable weather and pests. There is also a lot of distress selling to pay off loans taken to purchase seeds and fertilizer. The only way the rural income can grow is by giving the farmers remunerative prices for their produce. And to provide remunerative prices, we must increase the prices of agricultural produce. That would mean inflation. Thus if we want the rural incomes to increase along with the urban incomes, the prices of agricultural products must increase at the same rate at which the salaries of government servants increase and we must accept this inflation. Inflation is not acceptable to IMF. It is politically damaging. But we cannot keep 65 to 75 per cent of our countrymen in poverty just because inflation is inconvenient. If this 65 to 75 per cent of our population earned enough money to spend, the demand for all goods and services would grow and the economy would boom.

There is another aspect which bears looking into. This is related to purchasing power. Seen as a per cent of GDP, the manufactured goods are very cheap in the developed world. In the developing world, particularly in India, these products seen as per cent of per capita GDP are extremely costly and unaffordable to the average public. Hence the people in the developed world can afford to change these equipment quite frequently. In case of the average Indian these items are long-term buys. These goods may be used for 10 years or more. The consumption patterns of these products are completely different from the developed countries. However, the situation in the case of service industries is quite different. Let us see the purchasing power disparity:

| Product | Developed Country (Singapore) Per Capita GDP PPP 22,000 $ US or 880,000 India Rupee | | | India Per Capita GDP PPP 4000 $ or 160,000 Rupee | |
|---|---|---|---|---|---|
| | Cost in US $ | Cost in Rupee | % of GDP | Cost in Rupee | % of GDP |
| Economy Car | 8,000 | 3,20,000 | 36 | 2,00,000 | 125 |
| Personal Computer | 800 | 32,000 | 3.6 | 20,000 | 12.5 |
| Refrigerator | 200 | 8,000 | 1.1 | 8,000 | 5 |
| Washing Machine | 300 | 12,000 | 1.36 | 10,000 | 6.25 |
| House Rent* | 1,000 | 40,000 | 4.5 | 10,000 | 6.5 |
| Hair cut | 7 | 280 | | 20 | |
| Eating out, Self service | 5 | 200 | | 100 | |
| Plumber Charges | 50 | 2,000 | | 200 | |
| College Education# | 50,000 | 20,00,000 | | 50,000 | |
| Fresh Beef | 10 | 400 | | 40 | |
| Radish | 1 | 40 | | 10 | |

* Two bedroom flat in a condominium.
# per year cost at a professional college.

It will be seen that the difference in cost of different products and activities differ in an unacceptable manner between the developed and the developing world. The people of the developing world earn in local currencies. They pay for goods and services produced locally in the equivalent of the local currencies. These items are generally affordable. There are a few exceptions. These are items which have a good export market and are mostly exported. Thus prawns cost the same in Indian and developed country markets. But whatever is imported is priced in dollar equivalent and is extremely costly and unaffordable to the ordinary citizen.

This makes the issue of purchasing power parity of developing and developed world almost impossible. If these disparities are to be reduced, the people of the developing world must earn more and pay more. Paying more means inflation. But unless the consumer pays more, the producer cannot earn more. Thus the only way to reduce the disparity between the rich and the poor in the developing countries is controlled inflation with matching increase in incomes.

Unless there is some similarity in expenditure pattern in terms of percentage of per capita GDP globalization is neither possible nor desirable. It increases the disparity between the rich and the poor. Growth in terms of GDP has no meaning without reducing this disparity. Indonesia with a per capita GDP (PPP) of US $ 3750 has food riots. Bangladesh with a per capita GDP (PPP) of US $ 1000 has none. How does one explain the phenomena?

## Conclusion

Control of inflation in developing nations helps the developed nations to control their own inflation. If inflation is controlled in developing countries, the cost of imports of goods and services from the developing countries does not increase. In fact due to the constant devaluation of the currencies of the developing countries, the imports actually become cheaper. Consumers in the developed world have a ball. The population of the developing countries, particularly the rural population remain as poor as ever.

It should be obvious as to who gains from controlling inflation and why IMF insists on it. But does anyone in the developing world understand the implications of no inflation. We are too enamored of IMF and the developed countries to think differently.

# 9

# Foreign Exchange Management and the Developing World

## Economics of Domination

Has one ever wondered as to why Europe ruled and colonized the countries of Asia, Africa and America for centuries. The Indians claim that the Indian civilization is 5000 years old. The Chinese, Persian and Egyptian civilization are perhaps as old or at least contemporary. These countries were literate. They were well versed in art and sciences. They had developed their own calendars which were reasonably accurate. They had invented the wheel, knew enough of metallurgy to produce iron, gold, silver, copper and bronze. They knew enough about construction to construct such marvels as the Pyramids of Egypt, Hanging Gardens of Babylon, the Great Wall of China and the Taj Mahal. They had ships and traded their silks and spices long before European countries except Rome and Greece had set sail on the oceans. Yet these ancient civilizations failed to maintain their advantage. By the 17th century, European countries had taken over most of international trade and by the 18th century they had either colonized or controlled most of Asia, Africa and the Americas. By the 20th century, the rich nations of the first millennium had become poor and the underdeveloped countries of the first millennium, western and northern Europe had become the world rulers.

How did this happen? I am not a historian. But I feel that it is always necessary to look at history and learn lessons from it. Here are some of the reasons for the domination of the world by Europe (United States and Canada were colonies of Britain and France and are of the same people) as I see them.

- *Inhospitable terrain and climate*. The terrain and climate of much of Europe north of the Alps is inhospitable. The cultivable areas are restricted and the winters are bitterly cold. Survival was difficult. This made its people physically and mentally tough. It made them look at the riches of the developed countries of the first millennium, India, Persia and China with greed. They set out to find the legendary riches of India. In the process, they found the North and South Americas and colonized them. They found India and the Far East and colonized the countries. They found diamonds in Namibia and colonized it. They found gold and ivory in South Africa and colonized it. The list is the list of the developing nations.
- *Lack of natural resources*. Europe has most of the natural resources except oil. But the quantities are limited. As they industrialized, they felt the need for more natural resources. They crossed the seas and got them.
- *Human rights*. Feudal regimes were exploitive and encouraged exploitation of the working class and farmers by the priests and the hereditary ruling class. Literacy among the less privileged classes was discouraged as lack of education made exploitation easier. Serfs, slaves and other forms of bonded labor was common. The situation first changed with the proclamation of Magna Carta in England in 1215 which enshrined the human rights and constitutional rights of the common people and abolished serfdom and placed the ruler under the law of the land. The concept quickly spread to other parts of Europe and then to the United States. It led to the spread of education, improvements in the Human Development Index and growth in science and technologies in these countries. But the Feudal regimes of Asia and Africa did not change their ways.
- *Inventive skills*. Because of spread of education, science and technology developed faster in Europe and America.

They were the first to start the industrial revolution. They were the first to invent the musket and the cannon and exploited their superior weapons to the hilt in conquering the world. They have maintained their technological edge.

- *They had more nationalism.* Their leaders understood what was in the best interest of their countries. They pursued these interests relentlessly and they still do so. This is their hallmark. This is the secret of their success. They did not call in outside powers to help them settle their internal conflicts or their problems. They solved their own problems. That was not so in Asia and Africa. We always sought the military assistance of the European powers to settle our internal conflicts. In the process we were colonized.

The Asian and African Nations lack nationalism. Here decisions are made based on the interest of regions, tribes, caste, religion or the rich and the privileged. Our leaders either do not understand what is in the best interest of the country. Or they deliberately act otherwise to perpetuate narrow clannish, party or individual interests. We can only look in the short-term perspective like political and economic survival, for sectarian gains. The developed countries have no such problems. They know exactly what is their aim and what is in their best interest. They colonized the world for centuries. They gave up the colonies not because they wanted to. They found it too costly and messy to run the countries. Instead they developed a new tool for dominating the world. It was the route of economic domination. Domination of the world through the dollar, the IMF and the WTO. In India, thousands of years into history, Manu set up the caste system so that the privileged would always remain privileged, the rich will always remain rich and the poor will always remain poor. The developed countries have succeeded in doing the same. They have classified the world into developed and the developing worlds. They have built a world economic order that will ensure that the rich nations remain rich and the poor nations remain poor.

The tools of economic domination are simple:

- International trade will be in Dollars, Pounds, Yen or the Euro. Thus the wealth of nations will be decided by their holding of Dollars, Pounds, Yens and Euro. And as Dollar is the domestic currency of the United States, it will always remain the richest country in dollar terms. The developed countries will never be short of currency for trade.
- Domestic currencies of developing countries will have to be converted to the currencies of the developed countries if they want to purchase anything from outside their country. The exchange rate of the currencies of these countries with the Dollar, Yen and Euro will be determined by the developed countries through their currency markets based on so-called economic fundamentals. In simple words, it will be determined by the country's requirement of Dollars, Pounds, Yens or Euros to meet the cost of essential imports and debt repayments. Higher the requirement of hard currencies, the lower will be the conversion rate.
- The developing countries must allow unrestricted imports. This will ensure that their requirement of the hard will always remain high and the conversion rate will always remain low. This will ensure that the cost of imports into developed countries from the developing countries will in turn remain low. Less money will be required by the developed countries to invest in developing countries, to buy properties and companies.
- The developing countries will be able to earn hard currencies mainly through exports to America, Europe and Japan. Since all the developing countries will be desperate for earning hard currencies and the markets in the developed world are finite, the developing countries will keep fighting amongst themselves for a share in the export market. They will seek to make their products more competitive by making their products cheaper. However, the production cost in domestic currencies will

keep increasing over a period of time due to increasing labor and material costs. So to reduce the price in the international market, the developing countries will have to keep on devaluing their currencies. There will be tough competition between the developing countries. There will be price wars between the developing countries and constant reduction in prices. The developing countries will export more but earn less and less hard currencies. The developed countries and their consumers will benefit through cheaper imports. They will keep getting richer and the developing countries will keep becoming poorer.

- As the developing countries will always be desperately hungry for dollars and other hard currencies, the developed countries will be able to swing political decisions in their favor through the promise of loans, investments or grants in dollars and other hard currencies. Just as votes can be bought during elections in India through material inducements, the developed countries will be able to buy the votes of the developing nations in the United Nations or the WTO conferences. Their domination of the world, both politically and economically will be complete and perpetual.

Do the developing countries of this world want to be economic slaves of the developed world? If not, they will have to find a way to break the domination of the dollar and other hard currencies in their economies. They will have to stop fighting each other for exports to the markets of the developed world. They will have to stop devaluing their currencies and form cartels like the Oil Producing and Exporting Countries (OPEC) and get better values for their exports.

## Advantages and Disadvantages of Devaluation

Let us see the advantages and disadvantages of devaluation. The basic advantage of devaluation is that it makes exports cheaper and the basic disadvantage of devaluation is that it makes imports costly. Most developing countries export less than they import. Let us see an example:

**Trade Figures 2006 in Billion US $**

| Country | GDP PPP | Exports | Imports | Trade Deficit | Trade Deficit % of GDP |
|---|---|---|---|---|---|
| India | 4726 | 125 | 188 | 63 | 1.3 |
| Bangladesh | 360 | 10 | 14 | 4 | 1.1 |
| Mexico | 1249 | 248 | 253 | 5 | 4 |
| Vietnam | 297 | 20 | 22 | 2 | 6.7 |
| South Africa | 576 | 59 | 61 | 2 | 3.4 |
| Sri Lanka | 96 | 7 | 9.6 | 2.6 | 2.7 |
| Egypt | 388 | 14 | 24 | 10 | 2.6 |
| Philippines | 298 | 48 | 54 | 6 | 2 |

In 2006, 1 US $ was around rupees 40. If there was a 10 per cent devaluation in the Indian Rupee and the imports and exports remained the same in volume, the dollar cost of imports would go up to 206.8 billion US $ and receipts of exports will reduce to 112.5 billion US $. The current account deficit would increase to 94.3 billion US $. On the other hand if the Indian Rupee appreciated by 10 per cent and volumes remained the same, the cost of imports would be 169 billion dollars and the cost of exports would rise to 137.5 billion US $ and the trade deficit of 63 billion US $ would be halved to 30.5 billion US dollars. Even if the volume of exports dropped by 10 per cent due to the appreciation of the rupee by 10 per cent, the revenue from exports would be 124 billion US dollars and trade deficit will drop from 63 billion US $ to 45 billion US dollars. It will be obvious to the dumbest, that a strong currency will always be advantageous to those countries which have a trade deficit. The United States understands this fact much better than most other countries. That is why it spares no effort to maintain a strong dollar. Unfortunately most economists and finance ministers of most developing countries either do not understand this simple truth or opt for devaluation of the currency for some hidden motives like external aid or borrowings being converted to more local currency.

Devaluation of domestic currencies is not of interest to the developing nations. The concept of making exports more competitive through devaluation is seriously flawed. It only helps the exporters of the country and the consumers in the developed world. It never helps either the developing countries or their people. The consumption of any product in the world like tea, coffee, sugar is finite for a given population. Increase of exports by one country can only be at the cost of another. The developing nations must learn and understand that mindless competition amongst themself is only helping the developed nations get richer and making the developing nations poorer. Developing nations should not fight like street dogs for a piece of meat (the market of the developed world). They must learn to co-operate. If India, China and Sri Lanka produce 90 per cent of world tea, they must get together and control production and sale so that they get remunerative prices. If India and Australia produce 80 per cent of iron ore, it is in their interest to co-operate and ensure remunerative prices of their product. The volumes of exports may fall marginally in the short-term. But the returns in dollar terms will increase. We can either opt for over production and deflation like the OPEC countries have done and brought the price of crude oil to its lowest in 25 years from 1973 to 1998. Or we can co-operate and control production and get remunerative prices for our produce as OPEC countries have done in the period from 1999 to 2007 and taken the price of crude oil from $ 14 per barrel in 1999 to over $ 90 per barrel for most of 2007. By this simple manoeuvre, oil exporting countries are piling up their foreign exchange reserves and oil companies are posting record profits.

The pressure from IMF and the export lobby of the country for devaluation of domestic currencies of the developing countries will remain. The liberalization of imports and globalization is meant to ensure that. Economic fundamentals will not suddenly change. There will always be a shortage of dollars and other hard currencies to pay for imports and repayment of external debt. So if market forces are allowed to prevail, devaluation of the domestic currencies of the developing world will continue. If this is to be stopped, the developing nations must learn to co-operate. Barter trade must increase. Local currency trade between developing countries must increase. Imports must be reduced. The requirement of dollars and other hard currencies must be brought down. The developing nations must understand their national interests. They must learn to practice nationalism.

## Advantages and Disadvantages of Foreign Exchange Reserves

| Developing Countries with Large Reserves In billion $ US | | | | Reserves of G-7 Countries In billion $ US | | | |
|---|---|---|---|---|---|---|---|
| Country | Reserve | Imports | Reserves as % of Imports | Country | Reserve | Imports | Reserves as % of Imports |
| China | 1695 | 953 | 178 | US | 70 | 1869 | 3.7 |
| Russia | 484 | 226 | 214 | UK | 95 | 600 | 15.8 |
| India | 288 | 188 | 153 | Japan | 973 | 524 | 185 |
| Taiwan | 272 | 181 | 150 | Germany | 136 | 961 | 14 |
| South Korea | 261 | 356 | 73 | France | 115 | 529 | 21.7 |
| Brazil | 187 | 91 | 205 | Italy | 94 | 483 | 19.5 |
| Thailand | 115 | 119 | 96 | Canada | 41 | 404 | 10 |

It will be seen from the above figures that the developing countries hold far more foreign exchange reserves than the G-7 countries both in real terms and as per cent of imports. Japan is the only exception. Why is it so? I feel that developing countries have been psyched to believe that it is economically beneficial to have large foreign exchange reserves. Foreign Exchange reserves are required by countries whose currencies are other than the US Dollar, British Pound and Euro, mainly for imports, foreign investment, foreign debt repayment and foreign travel. China, Russia, Malaysia, Brazil and South Korea are countries with a trade surplus. Their foreign exchange reserves are almost redundant. India has a trade deficit of about 60 billion $ US. But this is made up to a large extent by other inflows like export of BPO and IT services, remittances, etc. and its foreign exchange reserve is growing every year. So what do you do with reserves?

Foreign currency cannot be use in the developing countries and even in developed countries except in the country to which the currency belongs. Thus the US $ cannot be used in Europe, Singapore or India unless it is converted to the local currency. It follows that the Indian Government cannot use the 288 billion US $ it has accumulated within the country. It can import what it wants with the foreign exchange. It can provide it in exchange for the India Rupee to Indians who go abroad for studies, tourism, medical treatment or any other purpose whatsoever. It can provide it to Indian companies against rupee loans or deposits for carrying out business operations and acquisition of foreign companies and real estate. It uses the foreign exchange to convert profits of multinational corporations to hards currency for repatriation. But even after doing all these things, the foreign exchange reserve is still growing. The government cannot use the vast sum of foreign exchange assets at its disposal to feed a single starving Indian. The situation is the same as that of a billionaire who has more money than he can spend. And like the billionaire, a developing country invests a major part of its foreign exchange. They invest most of the money in the US and Europe, in government bonds, in shares and other financial instruments and in real estate.

Let us try to understand the enormity of this ridiculous situation. The developing countries compete against each other, devalue their currency and earn the precious US $ by exporting garments, toys, commodities and raw materials. Then they go and invest the US dollars earned in the USA in US Treasury Bonds, real state or shares and thus, in reality, refund the money to the US, so that the US can give it back to the developing country by purchasing some more goods and services. This cycle of earning and refunding the US dollars US has been going on for over 50 years and still goes on. That is the big joke. The US, the world's biggest debtor nation with a foreign debt of over 1547 billion US $, or $79,000 per US citizen, can freely import any thing and every thing from the developing countries and continue to accumulate trade deficit of over 500 billion US $ per year. A developing nation with a foreign debt of 100 billion US $ is worried stiff as to how it is going to earn enough foreign exchange to repay the debt. The largest holders of US treasury bonds are Japan and China. Russians and Indians are the largest purchasers of real estate in London. And the US and UK can happily freeze these assets whenever they want to. Thus the US and UK and to a lesser extent the EU can have a cake and eat it too. Developing nations are so used to being exploited that they do not seem to have noticed the unfairness of the system. If they have, they seem to be reconciled to the continued exploitation by the developed countries. And that applies to economic power houses like China and India and a world power like Russia.

Let us look at another aspect of this unfair system. If the Indian Government invests 1 billion US $ in US Treasury Bond, the US government can use the money within the country. But if the US Government invests 1 billion US $ in Reserve Bank of India Bonds, the Indian Government cannot use the money within India. It has to be used only for import of goods and services.

## Conclusion

The consumers of the developed world will import what they want. Foreign exchange is not a constraint for them. Their domestic currencies are the foreign exchange the developing countries are willing to kill each other for. They cannot live without tea, coffee, rubber, meat, minerals and garments of the developing world. They will buy these products.

The consumers in the developing world must import what they need. They cannot afford to import what they may want to consume. Many of the developing countries do not have the foreign exchange to pay. If they fail to pay, their currency will be further devalued. So they will earn less from their exports and pay more for their imports. They will again fail to pay for the imports. Their currency will be further devalued. In 2001, 1 US $ was equal to 46.5 Indian rupees. In 30 years from 1971 to 2001, the value of the rupee has fallen to one fourth in dollar terms from Rupee 12 per US $ to Rupee 46.5 per US $. The situation of the currencies of the developing nations is similar. In some cases it is worse.

The poor developing nations with low foreign exchange reserves must aim to appreciate their currencies instead of devaluing them. To do that, they would have to reduce the demand for the dollar and other hard currencies. To reduce this demand, they will have to reduce imports. To reduce imports they have to restrict imports to essentials like petroleum products, technologies and food. To restrict imports, they have to get out of WTO. In other words, they will have to practice nationalism.

The developing nations must also understand that accumulating large foreign exchange reserves and then investing them in the developed countries only helps the developed world. They must learn to use their foreign exchange reserves better. They must decide how much foreign exchange reserve is required to be maintained to cater for imports and debt repayments. They must get rid of the surplus foreign exchange reserves by importing essential requirement of food, energy and technology. They must import whatever they need and try to use the foreign exchange reserves to benefit their own people. For example, Russia could import a 100 billion $ worth of Indian consumer goods and export an equivalent amount to India in terms of military hardware and nuclear reactors and in spite of the huge trade, their foreign exchange reserves will remain the same. Both countries will benefit immensely. The standard of living of the Russian people would improve as would the defense preparedness and availability of power in India would improve. Thus developing countries must trade with and invest in the developing countries rather than in the developed countries. They must try to increase barter and local currency trade. They must not accumulate unnecessarily large foreign reserves and learn to use the reserves to benefit the people of their countries. And their final goal should be to create a few new single currency zones like the Euro zone. Another possibility is to have a UN dollar rather than the US dollar as the vehicle of world trade. All countries including the US dollar should have a conversion rate with the UN dollar. So the developed countries will cease to have the unfair advantage of their currency being the currency for world trade.

By a stroke of good fortune and some suicidal economic policies of the United States which we will discuss in the next chapter, the value of the US Dollar has been falling. This should firm up the prices of commodities in $ terms. This could give great relief to the poor developing countries and reduce the economic domination of the developed world.

# 10

# Consumerism and the Developing Countries

## Consumerism

Consumerism is not consuming what is necessary to have an acceptable standard of living. It means conspicuous consumption, unnecessary consumption or addiction to shopping. It can also mean wasteful or excessive consumption. Eating a full meal is not consumerism. Taking a serving, consuming a part and trashing the rest is consumerism. Having dresses or shoes that we need is not consumerism. But having a hundred suits or a thousand pairs of shoes is. In the olden days, one got presents on one's birthday. The presents were things they could eat or use. Today we spend hundreds of dollars every year on various greeting cards which is a totally unproductive expenditure. That is consumerism.

When the state of economy is not measured by Human Development Index or by the absence of poverty but by per cent growth of GDP, consumerism assumes great importance. Consumerism sustains the developed world and their tools of mass production. In the US, the stock market rises and falls with consumer confidence. If cars were not frequently changed, how would new models sell and car sales grow. If fashions did not change every year and every season, how would sale of clothes grow. If there were no brands, how would the advertising industry thrive. If privacy went out of banking, how would crooks, despots, tax evaders survive, make money and consume. With stagnating or falling population growth, developed countries depend on growing consumerism to achieve GDP growth. They are also trying their level best to coax or coerce the developing countries to adopt consumerism as their way of life so their multinational corporations can make more profits by stoking the growing consumerism in the developing countries.

## Pillars of Consumerism

There are two pillars of consumerism, credit and media. To consume one must have money and it takes a long time to save enough to buy what one needs, let alone consume. In the late 'sixties, it took me seven years to save enough to buy a refrigerator. But in today's world you do not have to save money to buy almost anything. Banks and finance companies are falling over one another to give credit to anyone and everyone. For day-to-day consumption one has a credit card. For major purchase like cars or houses, there are banks and finance companies. So individuals are accumulating debt at a alarming rate. A young man or woman could have borrowed twenty years earnings for their house or ten months earning for his transport. So funding consumption is not a problem today for the urban middle class of developing countries.

The second pillar of consumerism is the media. The media with its round the clock advertisements is promoting an opulent lifestyle to promote consumption of consumer durables and other articles of consumption. It is also encouraging sexuality and free sex to increase sale of cosmetics and personal grooming facilities from beauty parlors to cosmetic surgeons and weight loss clinics. Even children are not spared the round the clock indoctrination to consume. "Shop till you drop" is made out to be the most enjoyable and desirable way to spend ones time and of course money.

## Sustainability of Consumerism

Should consumerism be encouraged just to generate demand? Can the developing nations afford to allow its people to follow western consumerism? Consumerism is gobbling up scarce natural resources of the world at a alarming rate. It is degrading the environment and polluting the world. Today

40 million tonnes of toxic waste is traded globally, most of it being passed on from the rich countries to the poor in the name of free trade. If consumerism of one fourth of the world population living in the industrially developed countries can create so much hazardous waste, what would happen if the whole world turned consumerist? Western consumerism is not sustainable. If India had one car per family, it would need 200 million cars. Is there road space for so many? Where would we get the fuel required for the 200 million cars? How will we earn the dollars to buy fuel for these cars? What kind of automobile pollution would it create ? What effect will it have on global warming and climate change?

Credit cannot sustain consumerism. Many economist would quote the US example to prove that credit fueled consumption is indeed sustainable. The US is the world's largest indebted nation with the per capita public debt amounting to about $80,000 or almost twice the per capita income of the US. The economists would proudly point out that in spite this massive debt, the US consumerism is sustaining the world economy. Is it really so? Excessive credit results in excessive debt and when the debtors fail to pay in large numbers for any reason whatsoever, economy goes into chaos. Loans are foreclosed. Cars and houses are repossessed. Banks and finance companies make losses. Every one suffers. The first time this happened was during the "Great Depression" of 1929. We have had a credit card default crisis in South Korea which required a few billion dollars bailout of the credit card companies. We have the sub-prime mortgage default crisis in the US which required about trillions of $ bailout from the US and European Central Banks. Only time will tell whether the bailout would be enough to revive the economy and stave off a serious recession in the US.

There is also a limit to human consumption. Bill Gates, no matter what his wealth, cannot consume more than 2 kilograms of food. He may have fifty cars but can use only one at a time. He may use his clothes only once and then discard them. But even then he cannot use more than 365 sets in a year. Free market and "Cowboy Capitalism" makes the rich richer and the poor poorer. It increases per capita consumption but reduces the number of consumers. The requirements of the "haves" are mostly satisfied. The "have nots" may want goods and services, but they cannot pay for them. So, if incomes of the majority of the population declines, consumption will also decline. The manufacturers of premium products may continue to make huge profits but the manufacturers of budget products will find their bottom lines coming under pressure. Consumerism is not sustainable unless more and more individuals of the country become prosperous.

Western consumerism is also not sustainable on the grounds of availability of resources. If the developing world were to match the per capita consumption of goods and services prevailing in the United States, crude oil, mineral and other resources of the world would prove to be totally inadequate to sustain such consumption in the long run. The emphasis needs to be on conservation rather than consumerism.

And finally there is the environmental angle. Consumerism in the western world has caused irreparable damage to the world environment. There is global warming. Forest cover is dwindling every year. Many edible species on our lands and in our seas are on the verge of extinction. Millions of tons of toxic waste are produced every year. Their disposal exposes the environment to new hazards. Higher the level of consumption, greater will be the level of environmental degradation.

Western style consumerism does not appear to be sustainable in developing countries in the long run. The developing nations do not have the foreign exchange to finance their requirement of imports. To enable them to import goods and services from the developed world, the developed countries either give them aid or loans. The loans may be directly given to a company or indirectly given to a government through the IMF or World Bank. There may be commercial credit or deferred payment schemes. The reality of the situation is that the developed countries are financing the purchase of their own goods and services with their own money. How long can the system work? Many of the developing countries have foreign debt which is two to ten times their foreign exchange reserves. Seventy-five per cent of the developing countries have a current account deficit. In other words, they import more than they export. From where will these countries get the foreign exchange to pay back the loans? Will the countries pay back through exports? What do they have to export? The products are generally agricultural products like tea, coffee, bananas, raw rubber, sugar, etc. How much of such products can the western world consume? To enable the developing nations to increase the export of such products to enable them to pay for their imports, a consumer in western countries will have to eat five bananas instead of one per day, change dresses every month instead of every year, drink ten cups of tea or coffee instead of five. Even that may not be enough to earn the required foreign exchange. Sooner than later these countries will start defaulting on foreign loans. That will hurt the foreign banks that have provided the loans. From where will the multinationals get foreign exchange to repatriate their profits? The entire world economy could be heading towards collapse.

## Conclusion

Developing countries must not be taken in by western.style consumerism. Not only is it not economically sustainable, it could lead to increase in crime and class wars between the haves and have nots. They must try to preserve their national and cultural values. They must realize that a country does not consist of a few cities and the urban rich. All citizens of the country have equal right to wealth and prosperity. They must have equal opportunity. It is not right to have economic policies which only suit the urban rich and their western style consumerism. They must realize that their state of development is a century to half a century behind the developed nations. It is not a handicap that can be made up with foreign aid in a few years, particularly if the population is as large and as backward as India is. Modern day wealth and prosperity can change quickly with devaluation of currencies, hyper inflation and collapse of the stock markets. You can gamble with your money but not with the lives of your people.

# 11

# Subsidies and the Developing World

## Nature and Type of Subsidies

Subsidy is a form of financial assistance paid, usually by the government, to keep prices of selected products and services below what they would be in a free market, to keep alive businesses that would otherwise go bust or to encourage consumption and activities that would otherwise not be possible for the poorer sections of the society. For example, the Government of India subsidizes food items and fuel which is distributed through its public distribution system and also education in government run or government aided institutions.

Subsidies can also be regarded as a form of protectionism or trade barrier which makes domestic goods and services cheaper than imports. It can also be used for promoting exports. The developed world uses subsidies of this type quite frequently. For example, Japan subsidizes the cost of domestically produced rice so that Japanese farmers do not have to compete against cheap import. The European Union on the other hand subsidizes the price of sugar produced in Europe so that it can compete in the world market against cheaper sugar produced by developing countries.

There are different kinds of subsidies. Direct subsidies involve a direct cash transfer to the recipient. For example, a subsidy paid to a fertilizer company per tonne of fertilizer sold to reduce its market price and encourage use of fertilizer by farmers. Indirect subsidy is a subsidy that is not directly paid to either the producer or consumer. An example of this kind of subsidy is the fixing the price of goods and services produced by Public Sector companies to benefit weaker sections of the society at the cost of profitability of the companies. Then we could have labor subsidies. This is a form of subsidy where the recipient, usually a company, receives subsidies to pay for labor costs.

A tax subsidy or tax break is another form of subsidy where the recipient, usually a company, receives the benefit through the tax system, usually through a rebate on income tax, profit tax or consumption tax. Examples of this kind of subsidy are tax breaks given by the US government to its companies, refund of sales tax to tourists visiting Singapore and 100 per cent depreciation to companies by Government of India on purchase of computers.

In certain cases governments may provide direct production subsidies to companies for production of a given good or service to encourage the development of a particular industry. For example, at one time Government of India gave money to companies which produced products which otherwise had to be imported. Governments may also provide subsidies to exporters to make the cost of exports competitive in the world market. These measures could include production subsidies, freight subsidies, reduction in duties and cash incentive payment in proportion to the exports achieved.

Governments everywhere are relatively large consumers of various goods and services. To reduce government expenditure, the government may subsidize goods and services which its departments procure. For example, for many years, government departments in India paid 4 per cent sales tax as against a sale tax rate of 7 per cent or more for private procurers. Many governments also provide consumption subsidies to boost their economy. In most countries, use of education, health care, and infrastructure like public transport are heavily subsidized and in some cases provided free of charge. In other cases, governments literally purchase or produce goods such as bread, wheat, gasoline, or electricity at higher prices than the cost of sale to the public. Such subsidies may require to target a particular group like students, people below poverty level, etc. to control the cost of providing the subsidy.

Another form of subsidy is due to the practice of a government guaranteeing a lender payment if a particular borrower defaults. This occurs in the United States, for example, in certain airline industry loans, in most student loans, in small business administration loans, in some mortgage backed bonds. A government guarantee of payment lowers the risk of the loan for a lender, and since interest rates are primarily based on risk, the interest rate for the borrower lowers as well.

### Pros and Cons of Subsidies

A view, held by many economists and neo-liberal capitalists, is that subsidies usually do more harm than good by distorting economic realities. Others believe that subsidies do not benefit the weaker sections but the rich and the corporations who bully governments with the threat of withdrawal from the market or stopping certain services unless they are subsidized.

Critics of agricultural subsidies believe that they result in poverty in developing countries by artificially driving down world crop prices. Agriculture is one of the few areas where developing countries have some production cost advantage. This makes developing countries into dependent buyers of food from wealthy countries rather than allowing the developing countries to develop their own agriculture and become self- sufficient in food production. Agricultural subsidies often are a common stumbling block in trade negotiations. The Doha Round of WTO trade negotiations continue to be stalled because the US and EU refused to cut subsidies to a level where other countries' non-subsidized exports would have been competitive. American critics also argue that agricultural subsidies go mostly to the biggest farms who need subsidization the least. Research from Brian M. Riedl at the Heritage Foundation showed that nearly three quarters of subsidy money goes to the wealthiest 10 per cent of recipients. Thus, the large farms, which are the most profitable because they have economies of scale, receive the most money.

## Subsidies and the Developed World

Developed countries, particularly the US and EU heavily subsidize their farmers and industries to protect them from competition from the developing world. Non Government Organizations (NGOs) like Oxfam describe such subsidies as dumping millions of tonnes of surplus commodities (like sugar) on world markets and thereby destroying opportunities for farmers in developing and poor countries, especially in Africa. For example, the EU is currently spending about 3 billion $ in subsidies to export sugar. These subsidies have remained in place even though many international accords have reduced other forms of subsidies or tariffs.

U.S. Agricultural Department is required by law to subsidize over two dozen commodities. Between 1996 and 2002, an average of $16 billion/year was paid by the US Government to its farmers. The beneficiaries of these subsidies have changed. In the 1930s, about 25 per cent of the country's population resided on the nation's 6,000,000 small farms. By 1997, 157,000 large farms accounted for 72 per cent of farm sales, with only 2 per cent of the U.S. population residing on farms. The subsidy programs give farmers extra money for their crops, as well as guaranteed minimum price. For instance in the 2002 Farm Bill, American farmers were paid an extra 52 cents for every bushel of wheat sold and guaranteed a price of 3.86 from 2002-03 and 3.92 from 2004-07. That meant that if the price of wheat in 2002 was 3.80 farmers would get an extra 58 cents per bushel (52 cents plus the $ 0.06 price difference). In 2004, the US Government paid a subsidy of 1.4 billion US $ to its cotton growers, about 1.2 billion US $ to wheat producers, 1.1 billion US $ to rice producers and so on. It spent a little over 8 billion US $ on farm subsidies. (*Source*: USDA 2006 Fiscal Year Budget)

## Subsidies and Developing Nations

Developing nations, with large sections of the society living below the poverty line, need to subsidize education, health care and infrastructure to ensure a decent standard of living for their people. But they are severely handicapped by their small budget to meet the needs of their people. And if they have taken loan from IMF on the condition of balancing their budget, they would not be able to subsidize what is necessary. The developing countries, therefore, need to be able to ensure that the benefits of subsidies reach the target segment of the society.

Fertilizer subsidy, fuel subsidy benefits the rich and poor alike. Cheaper fertilizer is supposed to reduce the price of food stuff which is consumed by the poor and the middle class alike. Distributing subsidized food stuff to Below Poverty Line (BPL) families will ensure that the subsidy reaches the target population and the cost to the exchequer is reduced. I have never been able to understand why petrol is subsidized in India. Petrol is used by cars and those who can by a car in a developing country do not need a subsidy. It is true that petrol is used in two wheelers which are used by the poorer sections of the society. To help them, petrol mixed with lubricants can be sold at a subsidized rate. Diesel needs to be subsidized to keep transport costs low. However, diesel cars should not be permitted. Not only does it results in the rich getting subsidized, it also results in higher levels of pollution. It is sad that governments of countries subsidize products used by the rich and the middle class but do not subsidize milk which is consumed by children. Education subsidy, free health care, midday meals are beneficial. Subsidized higher education is one of the reasons for India producing about one million engineering, medical and management graduates and other professionals per year and being the world's largest exporter of highly skilled professionals to the developed and developing countries. Midday meals draw children of poor parents to school and it has been a great success in India. Developing countries need to share their experiences with subsidies and ensure that their scarce financial resources benefit the weaker sections of the society and do not end up stoking consumerism of the rich and the middle class.

## Conclusion

It is naive to expect Japan not to subsidize its rice farmers and the developed countries not to act to save their farm sectors. US President Barak Obama has spoken against US jobs being and

I think he is right to do so. US pays $ 3 billion to 25,000 cotton farmers as subsidies. US paid another $ 12 billion in subsidies on other agricultural produces from corn to sugar to tobacco. A European cow receives $ 2.25 per day in subsidies while 75 per cent Africans live on less than $ 2 per day. The same will continue and may even increase. To survive, the developing nations must do all they can to prevent imports from developed world ruin their agriculture or industries. They must also realize that the developed world is not going to import their products to help the developing countries. They will only import what they need and export whatever they can. The developing countries need to focus on trade amongst the developing countries, specially balanced trade, to survive.

# 12

# Poverty and the Third World

## Difining Poverty

The poverty threshold or poverty line, is the minimum level of income needed to achieve an adequate standard of living. In practice the official or common understanding of the poverty line is significantly higher in developed nations than in developing countries. Almost all societies have some citizens living in poverty. Determining the poverty line is usually done by finding the total cost of all the essential resources that an average human adult consumes in one year. This approach is needs-based in that an assessment is made of the minimum expenditure needed to maintain a tolerable life. The poverty threshold is adjusted each year. In 2006, in the United States of America, the poverty threshold for a single person under 65 was US $10,488; the threshold for a family group of four, including two children, was US $20,444 or about one eighth of the per capita GDP.

Absolute poverty is a condition characterized by severe deprivation of basic human needs, including food, safe drinking water, sanitation facilities, health, shelter, education and information. It depends not only on income but also on access to services. David Gordon's paper, "Indicators of Poverty & Hunger", for the United Nations, further explains that absolute poverty is the absence of any two of the following eight basic needs:

- *Food:* Body Mass Index must be above 16.

- *Safe drinking water:* Water must not come from solely rivers and ponds, and must be available nearby (less than 15 minutes' walk each way).
- *Sanitation facilities:* Toilets or latrines must be accessible in or near the home.
- *Health:* Treatment must be received for serious illnesses and pregnancy.
- *Shelter:* Homes must have fewer than four people living in each room. Floors must not be made of dirt, mud, or clay.
- *Education:* Everyone must attend school or otherwise learn to read.
- *Information:* Everyone must have access to newspapers, radios, televisions, computers, or telephones at home.
- *Access to services:* This item is undefined by Gordon, but normally is used to indicate the complete panoply of education, health, legal, social, and financial credit services.

Another method of assessing poverty in the developing countries is people living below the per day income of $ 1 and $ 2 per day. Many Newly Industrialized countries like India have large percentage of their populations under the poverty line.

| Country | % below $ 1 per day | % below $ 2 per day | % below national level |
|---|---|---|---|
| Bangladesh | 41 | 84 | 50 |
| Bolivia | 23 | 42 | 62 |
| Cambodia | 34 | 77 | 35 |
| Ghana | 45 | 78 | 39 |
| India | 34 | 80 | 28 |
| Kenya | 22 | 58 | 52 |
| Nepal | 24 | 68 | 31 |
| Pakistan | 17 | 73 | 32 |
| Philippine | 14 | 43 | 37 |
| South Africa | 11 | 34 | 50 |
| Venezuela | 18 | 40 | 31 |
| Zambia | 63 | 87 | 68 |

It will be seen from the above figures that most of the developing countries have 30 per cent or more of their population below the national poverty line as against 10 to 15 per cent in the developed countries. It, therefore, becomes necessary for the governments of the developing countries to do their best to pull this section of their society out of abject poverty.

## Dealing with Poverty

The poverty of the developing countries, particularly of the third world is rooted in their exploitation during colonial rule. However, most of these countries have been independent over half a century. But their economic development has not been uniform. Some countries who have been led by good leaders and enjoyed relative peace have made good progress. Some have been let down by internal conflicts and poor leadership. Some common reasons for poverty in these countries are war or internal conflict, lack of employment, discriminatory policies where sections of the population are discriminated against them in government jobs and education, overpopulation. Overpopulation is another reason which leads to meager resources being shared by more people. In India less densely populated states like Rajasthan, Punjab and Gujarat have less poverty than densely populated states like West Bengal and Bihar. Lack of affordable facilities also contributes to poverty. Education improves skills and thus improves employability. In India, states with higher percentage of literacy and technical education like Kerala, Madras and Goa have less poverty than less literate states like Orissa, Madhya Pradesh and Uttar Pradesh. Poverty can also be due to cultural reasons. For example, certain ethnic classes like upper caste Assamese or Bengali's prefer to sit at home rather than do physical or blue collar jobs. As a result people from Bihar and Bangladesh fill up these employment opportunities.

Lack of infrastructure is perhaps the greatest impediment to development. Most developing nations suffer from inadequate infrastructure like roads, railways, electricity, schools, colleges, health care facilities and so on. Development of infrastructure automatically generates employment opportunities. Development of roads and railways lead to development of roadside facilities, petrol pumps, enable agricultural produce to reach the cities, development of different modes of public transport and enable rural population to commute to work at the cities and towns.

There cannot be an uniform approach to dealing with poverty in nations. For example the cultural, geographical and climatic conditions of the Nepal and Bangladesh are far too different for them to adopt the same approach. But there are many success stories which need to be studies and implemented where possible. For example, the micro credit system started in Bangladesh by a professor of economics has lifted thousands above the poverty line. The cooperative dairy development in Western India, the Prime Minister's Rural Roads Development program, the Mid Day Meal Scheme for school children in India etc. have yielded handsome results. Other countries must also be having their own success stories. The Developing Nations need to learn from and assist each other and reduce the levels of poverty amongst their people.

## Conclusion

We cannot allow the gulf between the rich and the poor, the urban and the rural to grow. We are not talking about equality. We are not talking about Communism or Socialism. We accept that nature is full of inequalities. We accept inequalities in distribution of wealth. But we also maintain that all people of all nations have a right to two square meals a day, a right to safe drinking water, a right to have a shelter over ones head, a right to work and earn and to live in dignity. All children and women of all nations must have the right to primary education and primary health care. Unless we can ensure that, there will be chaos. The people will not sit quietly and die of starvation. We have seen this in the French revolution. We see it today in the increasing levels of crime and lawlessness in our countries, in the food riots in Indonesia and India. We cannot rely on market forces to achieve that. Americans and their political leaders may not feel ashamed that over 4,00,000 Americans sleep in the streets, that about 38 million live below the national poverty line, that 15 million American children are growing up in poverty. I feel ashamed that about 800 million Indians do not have access to safe drinking water and toilets even after 60 years of independence. I feel ashamed for every man in the world who lives below the poverty line, for every child that is forced into child labor by hunger, for every woman who is forced into prostitution for survival, for every child and woman that is undernourished, for every infant that dies and every mother that dies at childbirth. That is where nationalism comes in. These problems are not going to be solved by globalization and liberalization and following the other tenants of neo-liberal capitalism. These problems will not be solved by frittering away scarce foreign exchange resources on import of whiskey, cigarettes, cars and cosmetics, televisions, music systems and refrigerators and establishing shopping malls and multiplexes instead of building infrastructure, educational institutions and health care facilities. The sooner we accept it the better.

# 13

# Globalization and Developing Countries

## Concept of Globalization

Globalization in economic terms implies a world free of all barriers to trade. It is a world economic order which does not recognize geographical boundaries or sovereignty of nations, particularly those of the developing nations. It is like a house without doors where the inmates have no right to close doors on unwanted visitors or to protect their wealth from robbers. Supporters of globalization want to turn the world into one global market. Globalization is designed to weaken the powers of individual Third World countries to control their own destinies and major decisions are increasingly made at the global level by WTO, IMF or World Bank. The influence of national governments is reduced. Actions by these countries to control their balance of payment or currency problems, if in contravention of the WTO rules can be referred to the WTO, which can impose hefty penalties.

The concept of Globalization of the world economy was thought out by the Washington Consensus to perpetuate US domination of the world economy. WTO was established to replace GATT as the international organization which is to govern world trade. The basic aim of economic globalization is to open up the entire world economy to imports of goods, services and capital from developed countries and their multinational corporations by removing trade barriers imposed by developing countries through import restrictions, duties and restrictions on inflow of foreign capital. The US is by far the richest country and controls the world economy with the support of its allies, bodies like the International Monetary Fund (IMF), World Bank and World Trade Organization (WTO) which it has created and controls and its multinational corporations. It wanted to manipulate the world economy so that it is adapted inextricably to suit the US and European investors and their multinational companies. The US does not believe in free trade in the US. It wants free trade only in developing countries. Free trade has been imposed on the poor countries by the leaders of the US and the developed world whose industries and commerce have been amply protected to ensure that the growth of US economy is assured. Under globalization most profits go to groups of American investors and American Multinational corporations and their European counterparts.

Globalization and associated liberalization of government control of commercial activity is the brain child of neo-liberal concept of capitalism and originated in Washington. The neo-liberals aim to reduce production costs by keeping the workforce insecure and easier to control. They are primarily concerned with cutting costs, raising salaries and incomes of the top management and maximizing profits for the owners and investors of multinational corporations. None of this is related to the needs of the workforce or the society. The neo-liberal theory of capitalism operates best when state intervention through taxes and controls is completely excluded. They demand that markets should be de-regularized, set free and allowed to find their own levels. Taxes and all forms of government control are seen as intrusion on free trade.

The impact of globalization so far has been to raise profits, strengthen the multinational corporations and weaken the workforce and governments. But in the new capitalist world order, it is the super rich elite group, most of them investors in the Third World countries who are the real beneficiaries. The system of exploitation has not changed from the colonial era. Rather it has become more extreme through the rapid growth of inequality.

## Problems of Globalization

Globalization has created more problems than it has solved. Most of the problems affect the poorer Third World countries. But some have affected the rich developed nations of the world.

*The first problem is the absence of level playing fields.* Modern neo-liberals of the Washington consensus recommend free trade and that all countries stop protectionism, reduce government controls and privatize the public sector including health-care. Yet most economic powers including America and the EU subsidize and protect their own industries and agriculture. Contrary to WTO rules, US and Japan also subsidize private research and development. The Third World, however, is not permitted to do such cheating. For them, the playing field is deliberately not level. The whole economic system has the effect of maximizing profit for the rich countries and for transnational corporations operating in them. It also maximizes the profits of investors living in the developed countries and minimize the economic benefits to Third World countries. Most third world countries are too weak to retaliate.

*The second problem of globalization is management of current account deficits and exchange rates.* It is a major problem with the debt ridden Third World economies. Adverse trade deficit can only be controlled by restricting imports. This is not permitted under globalization. To reduce budget deficit, countries cannot increase import duties. The only option available to the countries to earn foreign exchange to pay their debts is to sell their natural resources like iron or copper ores and agricultural products at throw away prices. The rich developed nations naturally benefit.

*The third problem is destruction of local industries and agriculture.* Cheap (subsidized) cotton from US is increasing the poverty of cotton growers in Brazil and Africa. Cheap (subsidized) sugar from EU is making it difficult for sugar growers in Africa and the Caribbean countries. Third World countries cannot compete with the quality and cost of many industrial products leading to closure of industrial units in the Third World. However, the situation is reversible. Cheap textile items and toys from China, Vietnam, India, cheaper and better cars, electronic items and household implement like refrigerators and washing machines, etc. are making it impossible for European and American industries to compete. This is leading to closure of some industrial units in those countries. Stoppage of subsidies could lead to closure of agricultural activities in the developed world leading to millions of farmers loosing their livelihood.

*The fourth problem is that quest for profit is the only motivation for economic action.* This effects rich and poor nations alike. In an environment with reducing government controls, the multinational companies rather than governments make investment decisions for establishment of manufacturing facilities. Because of availability of cheap labor and requirement of less investment, more and more transnational companies of developed countries are setting up production facilities or out sourcing facilities in developing countries. This is increasing their profits but leading to job losses in the developed world. Job losses in the developed world reduce their tax income and increase the burden on governments due to payment of unemployment benefits. The slow disappearance of well paid jobs in the developed world is working to the advantage of a few countries like China, India, etc. This is creating serious difficulties for the developed world.

*The fifth problem is that global economic growth has dropped over the last 25 years.* For the majority of the population, even in the US, wages have stagnated or declined in the last 25 years while working hours and insecurity has greatly increased. For a large portion of the world population conditions are awful and deteriorating and is most unsatisfactory. The correlation between economic growth and social welfare that had held in the post-war period has been severed after liberalization and globalization.

*The sixth problem arising out of globalization is growth of illegal migration and organized crime.* Thirty per cent of the world population is unemployed. Opportunities for employment and growth are severely restricted in many of the Third World countries. This leads to desire of the youth of these countries to migrate to the West. However, immigration is strictly controlled.

So a nexus has developed between unscrupulous businessmen looking for cheap labor (illegal immigrants can be hired for half the cost) and organized crime and human trafficking is on the rise. Other crimes like smuggling of drugs and money laundering also thrives in the globalized environment.

*The seventh problem is that price liberalization is a part of the globalization package.* Price liberalization implies that governments will not control prices of agricultural products, commodities, medicines, etc. They will allow prices to be determined by market forces. This tends to produce substantial rise in the domestic prices of fertilizer, farm inputs and equipment which have an immediate effect in most areas of economic activity in the Third World the bulk of whose population are dependent on agriculture for their livelihood.

*The eighth and perhaps the most important problem is the growth of inequalities.* The forces of neo-liberalism are trying to turn the clock back more than two hundred years, to the beginning of industrial revolution by abolishing worker rights and bring back the social conditions of Blakes *Dark Satanic Mills* or Charles Dickens' *David Copperfield.* The neo-liberals aim to get rid of the welfare state for the workers, even though this would produce desperation, anxiety, hopelessness and fear. The accumulation of wealth has been extraordinary. In 1996, United Nations Development Program (UNDP) reported that the assets of 358 billionaires of the world exceeded the combined incomes of 45 per cent of the world's population. By 2005, it must have crossed 50 per cent.

## Future of Globalization in the US

Chomsky, the noted thinker and critique of US foreign and economic policies says that just as the cold war was the defining issue for the 20th century and colonization was the defining issue of the 18th century, the defining issue of the 21st century is going to be globalization. Success or failure of globalization will, therefore, have a great bearing on the rise or fall of the US. It appears that the forces of globalization unleashed by the US, at the behest of their powerful multinational corporations and the lobbies for short-term economic gains are going to prove similarly disastrous in the long run. Like the war on terror, globalization is not succeeding for the US. While the national income has been growing, the economic prospects of most Americans have been diminishing. For the vast majority of working Americans, real hourly wages have fallen significantly over the last 25 years. What supporters of globalization ignore is the frightening growth of low wage jobs. As a result 30 per cent of the population of the country are earning too little to lift a family out of poverty. Globalization has not reversed the pattern of poverty for 30 per cent Americans. It is only accentuating it.

> "Italy is particularly vulnerable because so much of our industrial production comes from mid level to relatively low technology and also because of the high cost of Labour.
>
> "My position isn't against the Chinese. They look out after their own interests, and Europe should simply do the same.... We have too many rule coming from Brussles on business. There is an almost obsessive quantity of rules. Yet we freely import from countries which do not have any of these rules."
>
> —Italian Finance Minister Guilio Tremonti warns about the down side of unbridled free trade with China in an interview with Times Magazine.

The Third World countries like China, India, ASEAN countries, South Africa, Brazil and some other Latin American and African countries have come together to resist US and EU economic hegemony. It is acknowledged by the discerning that economic power is shifting towards the top economic performers amongst the developing countries. With domestically available cheap and highly skilled workforce and cutting edge technology from the transnational corporations from the developed world, their products are more competitive than products produced in the developed world. Thus factories producing cars are closing in the US and opening in China and India. In fact even high-tech services like Information Technology, research and development, health care, business processes are being increasingly outsourced to the so-called Third World countries. There is no doubt that

US transnational companies will continue to make substantial profits. But the US economy will suffer from the millions of job losses that are bound to occur.

## Conclusion

Globalization is a concept developed by the developed nations for the benefit of the developed nations. It is their answer to the lack of demand in their own countries to sustain the production capacities which have been created. Globalization is a ploy to exploit the developing world with money of Western investors in the same way the moneylenders have exploited the poor in our countries for centuries by slowly taking over their assets and finally making them economic slaves. Let us not be taken in by the jargon and the hard sell. There is no truth in the promise of universal prosperity through globalization. Capitalism ensures that the rich get richer and the poor get poorer. It is true for individuals. It is true for nations. The sooner the developing countries understand it, the better.

Unfortunately, the concept of globalization cannot survive in the long run. The Doha round of trade negotiations are likely to fail. The US and EU will find it extremely difficult to abolish farm and export subsidies. Abolishing these subsidies could be fatal for the developed world. And without this commitment the G 24 are unlikely to relent. So, further globalization will stop. But manufacturing industries of the world have already shifted to the Newly Industrialized countries and they will hold the competitive edge. General Motors of US is on the brink of bankruptcy. The poorest nations have already been milked to the bone. The US cannot extract any thing more out of them. Globalization will enrich certain Third World countries and weaken the economies of US and the developed world. The balance of economic power could decisively swing to Asia in the 21st century.

Predatory capitalism that globalization represents is not a fit system for the 21st century. It is incapable of meeting the human needs that can only be expressed in the collective terms and in the concept of competitive man who seeks only to maximize wealth and power, who subjects himself to market relationship, to exploitation and external authority. In a globalized world, it is some how seen as right and proper that the winner should become enormously rich whereas the looser ends up on the bread line. Since the global economic system is based on profit, inequalities are normal, natural and desirable. But inequalities bring conflicts in its wake. And conflicts are bad for economic growth.

Globalization is yet to bring higher standards of living to the ordinary population of most countries. Indications are that it will not do so. The increasing gap between the rich and the poor is likely to result in social unrest of the kind we saw sweep many poor suburbs of Paris and other towns of France in November 2005. Like many other strategies born out of capitalist greed, globalization is bound to fail. It will only work if it is restructured to benefit the people of the world rather than multinational corporations and the developed world. It will work when it can reduce rather than increase inequalities.

# PART II

# MODELS FOR DEVELOPMENT

# 14

# Capitalism

## History of Capitalism

Capitalism has been called the natural economic order of mankind and perhaps rightly so. It evolved with mankind and was reformed with the evolution of society and the needs of commerce, industry and growth. Capitalism is about an individual's right to property, to wealth, to the profits of his enterprise and ingenuity. It started with commerce in agricultural products and manufactured goods on barter basis. Then came the coins, the paper money and other forms of legal tender. The governments, the kings to start with, collected taxes on this trade and commerce. Since the traders and entrepreneurs were a source of revenue, they received encouragement from the kings in the form of protection from robbers, development of infrastructure like roads, ferries, ports, rest houses, market places and so on. Their need for finance was met by moneylenders and kings. The kings also enacted laws and settled disputes. As time went by, technologies developed and volumes grew. To keep pace with it came new infrastructure, new financial institutions, new financial systems.

Capitalism unleashed its productive forces with the advent of industrial revolution and mass production in Europe in the 13th century. It also created two classes of people, the owners of means of production and the workers or the wage earners. The owners of the means of production, whether individuals or companies, became immensely rich and powerful. They felt that profits were more important than human right and fair play. They exploited the wage earners to the hilt. To reduce cost and increase profits, they used child labor and paid minimum possible wages. Working conditions and safety standards were appalling. Slaves and bonded labor became the order of the day in the colonies. Protests were put down by influencing the law enforcers and local officials. Natural resources were ruthlessly exploited. Forests were cut down. Hazardous industrial waste was indiscriminately released into water channels and the sea with irreparable damage to the environment. When the exploitation reached unacceptable levels, labor began to organize themselves. Unions began to be formed. Socialist and communist ideologies began to take shape and influence government. Laws regarding prevention of use of child labor, maximum working hours, minimum wages, safety standards, welfare measures and compensations for death or injury while working came into force. Environment protection laws had to be enacted to protect the environment. Consumer protection laws were enacted to protect the consumers from exploitation. However, there are no laws to protect the interests of the developing countries. Thus, by the beginning of the 20th century, exploitation of the working class had been controlled to a large extent in most of Europe and the US. However, exploitation of labor continiued in the colonies. Thus capitalism ruled the world unchallenged from the beginning of civilization till the end of the Second World War.

Capitalism had come under threat from Communism after the Bolshevik Revolution of 1917 and the formation of Communist and Socialist Parties in the US and Europe. After the world war, most of the European countries introduced welfare measures to ensure a decent and dignified life for their citizens. These measures are discussed in the next chapter.

Right through the period since the industrial revolution, the companies owning the means of production and services like railroads, construction, airlines had become richer and more powerful. These multi billion dollar behemoths chaffed at the controls placed on their exploitive activities. They used their financial clout to influence the Republican Party of the US to usher in their neo-liberal ideology into Capitalism. Thus when President Ronald Regan came to power in the US, he abolished many welfare measures and controls on multinational corporations introduced by President Roosevelt under his "New Deal". His example was followed by Mrs. Margaret Thatcher in Britain. Robert J. Samuelson, the noted economist has described neo-liberal Capitalism as holding "profit" as its god and "greed" as its sustaining religion.

The controls imposed on the companies, mainly multinationals, and entrepreneurs within the developed world reduced profits. They promptly shifted their operations to the developing world where the labor was cheap, consumer protection laws either did not exist or were weak, the labor and environmental laws were non-existent or poorly implemented or circumvented by bribes. Thus pesticides and medicines banned in the developed world are freely sold by the multinationals in the developing world. The companies and individuals prospered at the cost of the local population. The rich western nations became richer.

Capitalist system believes that economic activity should decided set by price signals in the market place. It expects and depends upon quest for profit to be the only motivation for economic action. But extreme capitalism as desired by neo-liberals does not cater to the needs of the weaker sections of the society. It also leaves governments too weak to effectively respond to natural calamities like drought, floods, earthquakes or hurricanes. A common argument in favor of unregulated trade is that it will lead to general rise in living standards. Experience has shown that opening up of trade and financial markets benefits only a small group. Investors, entrepreneurs and professionals have made a lot of money but many of the poorer countries have been victim of a marked drop in living standards. The third world has suffered considerably under globalized free trade and it is possible that the leadership of the Third World are at last beginning to understand the true situation. Trading glass beads for gold will become difficult with spread of education and exposure.

## Is Wealth of Developed Nations Due to Capitalism?

Is it correct to accept that the wealth of the Western Industrialized nations is solely due to capitalism? Let us look at some hard facts.

Europe colonized most of the world from the 17th to the 20th century. Spain plundered all the Inca and Maya gold and ruled much of Mexico, Central and Latin America. Britain, France, Germany, Holland, Italy and Portugal colonized most of Asia and Africa and took complete control of trade and commerce in these countries. They took billions of dollars worth of gold and jewelry as compensation and taxes from the defeated countries. Many of the British crown jewels had adorned Indian crowns. They took over and exploited the natural resources of these countries like minerals, spices, tea, coffee, rubber, ivory and silks with minimum possible compensation. It brought them great riches and left the colonies in abject poverty and a state of underdevelopment.

In America the local Red Indian population was driven off the lands into reservations without any compensation. Today we protest against ethnic cleansing in Yugoslavia. Has there ever been a greater example of ethnic cleansing in the world as compared to the U.S. Perhaps only in Australia where the Aborigines have been decimated. Is it also not true that most of the economy of the southern states of America were developed with the help of slaves from Africa at almost no cost at all? Slaves from Africa and bonded labor from India were extensively used in sugar, banana, coffee, tea and rubber plantation in the Carribeans, South America, Africa and Asia and South Pacific Islands. Is American and European wealth solely the result of capitalism? England fought and won a war with China for the right to sell opium. It not only made great wealth from this narcotic trade but also obtained the territory of Hong Kong and compensation for the war. Was this wealth obtained through capitalism? Is it not ironic that US and Britain are condemning Myanmar, Thailand, Afghanistan and Columbia for not doing enough to stop the cultivation and export of narcotics. In India, the British forced the farmers of Bengal and Bihar to cultivate Indigo instead of rice.

It did not matter that many starved and there was a famine in 1942. What mattered was the British companies made handsome profits. Is it also not true that the British cut off the thumbs of the Muslin weavers of Bengal because the cloth manufactured in Britain could not match the local fabric "Muslin" which they produced? It did not matter that the weavers starved. What mattered was that British cloth produced in Manchester could be sold and British companies made good profit.

It should be quite obvious that the wealth of the Western Economies is not purely as a result of Capitalism. Much of it is due to barbaric acts and practices which would not be acceptable in today's world. History cannot be reversed. But an essential fact which developing nations must clearly understand is that the developed world has developed at our cost. They plundered the riches of our kings. They exploited our mineral resources without any compensation or royalties. They have a head start. And since, in Capitalism the rich must get richer and the poor will get poorer, it is unlikely that the developing world will be able to narrow the gap through the vehicle of western capitalism. It is interesting to note that out of 89 nations under IMF care between 1965 and 1995, 16 stagnated and 32 became poorer.

## Crisis of Capitalism

Might is right and survival of the fittest are the laws of the wild. They are not the laws of a modern society where rule of law must prevail, where human beings have rights and social justice has to prevail. Significantly, Capitalism was not always practiced as it is today. Social welfare and social justice was very much a part of the Capitalist system that existed only a couple of decades ago. It vanished with the introduction of Reganism and Thatcherism. Today's neo-liberal Capitalism is a set of rules shared by the leaders of the World Bank, IMF and the United States Treasury and the multinational corporations they represent. The neo-liberals want the corporate world to be freed of government controls and regulations. They want taxes and tariffs to be abolished or reduced. They want free flow of capital and investments to be allowed across the globe. They want prices to be deregulated and left to be evolved at the market place based on demand and supply.

Neo-liberal Capitalism is not working very well for the developing countries. The first problem is "Hot Money". Today's technology allows billions of dollars of short-term investment in stock markets to flow in and out of the countries at the press of a computer button. Such flows can create havoc with the economies of the developing countries by wiping out foreign currency reserves and leading to devaluation of currencies, loss of investor confidence, drop in share and property prices, increase in non-performing assets with banks, bankruptcies, job losses and depression of demand. One such collapse started in Thailand in June 1997 and quickly followed through the other South East Asian Economies like that of Hong Kong, Singapore, Malaysia, Philippines, Indonesia, etc. The air traffic in South East Asia fell by 40 per cent. Philippine Airlines was on the verge of collapse. Malaysia was selling off its aircraft. Tourist trade was drastically reduced. Millions lost their jobs. Consumption, the sustaining force of Capitalism went down. The effect was not confined to the developing world. The western world also faced problems. Boeing had some of its aircraft orders canceled. US exports fell 8 per cent. Multinational corporations found their profitability shrinking. Manufacturing units in the developing world were finding it difficult to sell their products. Every one was hurt. It took the world about five to six years to recover from the down turn.

Russia has given up its flirtation with Capitalism after the traumatic collapse of its economy that left its middle class shell shocked and financially ruined. Under Prime Minister Primakov it introduced vast increases in subsidies to industry, restricted imports and instituted Soviet era type controls on foreign exchange convertibility. Nationalism practiced by Russia under President Putin aided by high oil prices have reversed the downward trend and put Russian economy on the road to recovery. From being forced to borrow billions of dollars from IMF to survive, today it has a foreign exchange balance of about 400 billion US $.

China seems to have gained remarkably through liberalization of its economy. In its first twenty years of economic reforms from 1978 to 1998, its per capita GDP had grown from 379 Yuan to 6431 Yuan. Trade during the period increased from US $ 20.6 billion to US $ 319 billion. Foreign exchange reserves rose from US $ 167 million to about a trillion and a half US $ by the end of 2007. The figures are most impressive. What is often forgotten is that China never adopted neo-liberal Capitalism in its totality. It has strict capital controls and a controlled foreign exchange conversion regime. The free market access to foreign companies is restricted to a few coastal regions and towns and having Chinese companies as partners is often mandatory for investing multinational corporations. Thus the Chinese economic reforms are more nationalist than capitalist. A toothbrush I recently brought carried the "Colgate" brand name and design. It was made by a Chinese company in China, packaged by an Indian company in India and sold in India at a discounted price. But China, in spite of its remarkable success, is not free from internal problems. China has backed away from the toughest part of the reforms. Fearing that the resulting unemployment will fuel unrest and instability, its leadership have decided against closing down loss making state enterprises and decided to recapitalize and modernize them. Housing subsidies have been retained and privatization of housing development postponed.

### Neo Capitalism is Failing

The United States is the capital of capitalism. It is the fountain head of Neo Liberal capitalism, of free markets. But it is in deep economic crisis. Many pillars of US capitalism are in trouble.

*Housing industry is in trouble.* The US housing industry was on a roll till 2006 on the back of easy credit. The sudden tightening of credit on high-risk sub-prime mortgages has led to a property price crash in the US, with devastating effects on the whole economy. The unprecedented decline in US house prices may also lead to further pain for financial institutions, who collectively own more than $ 1 trillion worth of sub-prime debt. "This is the first time we have had an absolute decline in housing prices in the US market since the Great Depression"—Richard

Syron, Chairman, Freddie Mac (a financial services company). The magnitude of the collapse has surprised experts. There is nearly a year's supply of unsold houses standing vacant. Mark Zandi, an economist at Moody's, who is tracking the housing market, expects the fall in house prices to accelerate from 5 per cent in 2007 to 10 per cent in 2008. He says that prices could end up 10-15 per cent lower than the peak of 2006 if policymakers move quickly to stem the wave of foreclosures. But if they don't, and if interest rates are forced up by the inflationary worries, he says prices could fall by 15 per cent to 20 per cent. Mr. Zandi identifies three factors that have caused the property crash, speculative purchase of homes by investors, the availability of easy credit, where mortgages were granted to people who could not really afford them and the over-supply of new houses by builders. The National Association of House Builders' chief economist, David Sieders, has warned that house building would contract by 50 per cent in the next two years, cutting employment by 1-2 million jobs and wiping out many firms. He fears that prices might not start rising again until 2010. A wave of foreclosures and evictions is sweeping the United States in the wake of the sub-prime mortgage lending crisis. This could destabilize the US housing market and may also lead to further turmoil in financial institutions, who collectively own $1 trillion worth of sub-prime debt.

*US manufacturing is in trouble.* US manufacturing has been on the decline for some time but the US government and much of the media has not drawn too much attention to it. The employment in this sector fell from 17.5 million in 1997 to 14.2 million in 2006. In other words, the US lost 3.3 million highly skilled well paying jobs during these ten years. The decline is expected to continue at the rate of 1.1% for the next ten years.

*US service industry is in trouble.* US consumerism is in the decline. During the last quarter of 2007, unemployment rate rose from 4.7 per cent to 5 per cent. The US service sector shrunk for the first time in five years.

*Major banks of US, UK and Europe are in trouble.* The world's largest banks have already admitted losing more than $100bn from mortgage bonds gone bad. The main sub-prime losses reported in the third quarter of 2007 are Citigroup: $ 18bn, UBS: $ 13.5bn, Morgan Stanley $ 9.4bn, Merrill Lynch: $ 8bn, HSBC: $ 3.4bn, Bear Stearns: $ 3.2bn, Deutsche Bank: $ 3.2bn, Bank of America: $ 3bn, Barclays: $ 2.6bn, Royal Bank of Scotland: $ 2.6bn, Freddie Mac: $ 2bn, Credit Suisse: $ 1bn, Wachovia: $ 1.1bn, IKB: $ 2.6bn, Paribas: $ 197m (*Source:* Company reports). US banking giant, Citigroup has reported a $ 9.83bn net loss for the last three months of 2007. The company, the largest banking group in the US, said revenues during the fourth quarter fell 70 per cent from a year earlier to $ 7.2bn. Mr. Prince, the Chief Executive resigned in November after the full extent of Citigroup's sub-prime mortgage losses began to emerge. (Citibank was founded in 1812 in New York. It has 200 million customer accounts in 100 countries, more than 300,000 employees and $ 2.4 trillion in assets.) US bank J.P. Morgan Chase has said its earnings for the last three months of 2007 fell 34 per cent as a result of its exposure to soured US mortgage loans. The bank said it had to cut the value of investments linked to the US mortgage market by $ 1.3bn. Wells Fargo, the biggest bank on North America's West Coast, said the home loans crisis had led to its first drop in quarterly profits since 2001 and reported a 38 per cent decline in net income to $ 1.36bn for the last three months of 2007. Wall Street banking giant Merrill Lynch has unveiled a huge loss for 2007, crippled by exposure to risky investments in the US housing market. The loss includes a massive $ 14.1bn write-down on failed investments related to sub-prime mortgages. Merrill Lynch is the latest big bank to reveal losses related to the crisis in the US mortgage market. In the last three months of 2007 alone, Merrill chalked up losses of $ 9.83bn, the biggest quarterly loss in its history. The previous chief executive, Stan O'Neal, stepped down in October because of the bank's poor performance. BBC Business Editor Robert Peston said that Merrill has avoided bankruptcy because of lifesaving capital injection from the cash-rich economies of Asia and the Middle East.

*Other Financial Services like mortgage companies and bond insurers are in trouble.* The sub-prime (mortgage) market of the US is focused on providing home loans to those with limited or poor credit histories. Many of these mortgages were converted into financial instruments and sold on to investors including banks. But a series of interest rate rises over the past two years has meant many sub-prime borrowers could no longer afford their monthly payments, causing them to default. This led to a steep fall in the value of investments linked to sub-prime loans and has caused many banks to report massive losses. As a result many mortgage companies in the US and UK are close to bankruptcies. The largest mortgage company in the US, Countrywide has been taken over by Bank of America while the British Government has poured billions of pounds of taxpayer's money into the British Bank, Northern Rocks, to save it from going bankrupt. Bond insurers are also in trouble. Analysts at Barclay's Capital said banks own $ 820bn of securities guaranteed by bond insurers. After insuring debt hit by the sub-prime mortgage crisis, bond insurers, such as Ambac Financial Group and MBIA, have suffered billions of dollars of write-downs in recent months. They are expected to sustain more losses. Many investors fear that the insurers have too little capital to meet their obligations and worry that a cut in the credit rating of bond insurers would make it more expensive for them to borrow money. Ratings agency Fitch cut Ambac's rating in January 2008 while rival agencies Moody's and Standard & Poor's are reviewing Ambac's and MBIA's ratings.

*The US dollar is falling.* The US has been running massive current account and budget deficits during most of the Bush Presidency. It has stopped intimating the amount of currency it is printing, a clear indication of large scale deficit financing. Federal Debt at 9.2 trillion US $ is at an all time high. Given such adverse economic indicators, the mighty US dollar is falling. This can be seen from price of gold. In 1997, the price of gold was about 250 $ US per oz. By March 2008, the price had reached a peak of 992 $ US per oz. During the period the US $ has decline against the British Pound and particularly the Euro.

| Currency/$ US | 2007 | 2006 | 2005 | 2004 | 2003 | 2002 | 2001 | 2000 | 1999 | 1998 |
|---|---|---|---|---|---|---|---|---|---|---|
| Euro | .757 | .738 | .793 | .953 | 1.12 | 1.06 | .99 | .85 | | |
| Pound | .51 | .58 | .52 | .56 | .62 | .698 | .694 | .659 | .618 | .60 |

In January 2008, the US $ dropped to a 26-year low against the British Pound. The US $ has also decline against the currencies of the developing world. In 2005, 1 US $ was equal to about 48 Indian Rupees. Today it is equal to about 39.50 Indian Rupees. If the US dollar is getting devalued, can inflation be far behind.

*Poverty is increasing in the US*

It is baffling that the world's richest nation has over 10 per cent of it population living below the poverty line. In comparison the people below poverty line in France is 6.5 per cent, South Korea 4 per cent, Malaysia 8 per cent and Thailand 10 per cent. Let us look at the figures below which have been obtained from the website www.census.gov:

| Year | 1992 | 1994 | 1996 | 1998 | 1999 | 2000 | 2001 | 2002 | 2003 | 2004 |
|---|---|---|---|---|---|---|---|---|---|---|
| % below poverty level | 13.3 | 13.1 | 12.2 | 11.2 | 10.3 | 9.6 | 9.9 | 10.4 | 10.8 | 11.0 |

When President Bush Senior handed over to President Clinton in 1992, the American people living below poverty line was 13.2 per cent. At the end of the Clinton Presidency it was down to 9.6 or a fall of 3.6 per cent. In other words Clinton managed to pull over 12 million Americans above the poverty line. Under President Bush, the trend has reversed. People below the poverty line have increased by 1.1 per cent. In other words, about 4.5 million Americans have fallen back below the poverty line since 2000. This has happened at a time when the GDP is supposed to be growing at over 3 per cent. In a nation of nearly 300 million people, the number living below poverty line ($ 14,680 for a family of three) recently hit 37 million, up more than a million in the year. In fact ever since 2000, one million Americans are falling below the poverty line every year. Is this a sign of the triumph of capitalism?

## Capitalism is in Trouble in Western Europe

If the US is the capital of capitalism, Western Europe is its cradle. But here also economy is not doing too well. European Banks to have invested heavily in the US mortgage market and speculative instruments in search of large profits. They have not escaped the US sub-prime crisis. The largest Swiss bank UBS has written off 14 billion US $ worth of bad debts and is expected to report a $ 4 billion net loss for 2007. The second largest French bank, Societe Generale reported a loss of $ 7.38 billions in a banking scandal resulting from uncontrolled speculation. The incident reminds one of a similar incident in Barings Bank of UK in 2002. Banks world-wide have announced more than 135 billion US $ losses and write downs up to 1 February 2008 due to the turmoil in housing market in the US in 2007. Some analysts believe that the total write downs could reach 800 billion to 1 trillion US $ by the end of 2008. The British economy is also showing signs of strain. British manufacturing has been in decline for almost two decades. The property prices in UK appear to be falling. The US sub-prime crisis has affected British banking sector. The loss making Norther Rocks had to be nationalized to prevent it from going bankrupt. The HSCB, the largest British bank admitted to losing 17.6 billion US $ in the crisis.

## Reasons for Failure of Neo-Capitalism

The interest of the developed countries and their multinational companies are often made out to be the same. But in actual fact they are not. When a multinational makes profits, the developed countries get taxes from it. But countries have responsibilities towards their people. They have to ensure that the population of the country can maintain or improve their standard of living. If they fail, the government in power is liable to be thrown out at the next election. Governments have to ensure the soundness of their banking systems and other financial institutions. But the multinational corporations have no such responsibility. They can lay off thousands of workers whenever they feel like and leave it to the government to foot the bill of unemployment benefits. They can shift their manufacturing to the Third World and increase their profits by exporting these products to the markets of their parent countries. In the process they cause job losses in the developed world and increase trade deficit. Both cause serious economic and humanitarian problems in the developed countries. If a bank or multinational company goes bankrupt, the management never suffers. They have seen it coming and taken out their investments well before the collapse. Through some creative accounting or fraud, they may have even shown large profits and taken millions of dollars as bonus. The collapse of the US multinational energy behemoth Enron in 2002 is an example. The employees, small investors and the depositors of the banks suffer. Any compensation for them becomes the responsibility of the government. Cuts in taxes of multinational corporations in the US are not going to generate jobs in the US but in the Third World. Interest cuts are not going to be passed on by struggling banks to their customers. It will only help the multinational corporations and investors to borrow more money and invest it in the Third World. It is amazing that this simple economic logic does not seem to be understood by the learned economists and central banks of the developed world.

The surplus capital with the large investors of the developed world is also causing problems. The investor has to find an avenue for investing his surplus capital and make more money. This investment can create two problems. Too much money with too few avenues of investment creates bubbles which are very painful when they burst. The Asian property bubble of 1997-98, the "Dot.com" bubble in the US of 2002 and the Housing Bubble of 2007 in the US are some recent examples. The second problem which is also very painful is investment in high risk financial instruments like the housing bonds which went bad due to the sub-prime lending crisis in the US and derivatives markets and hedge funds which collapse when there is abnormal fluctuations in the currency markets or share markets for a sustained period. In both cases, the governments and their central banks are left holding the babies and trying to sort out the mess. Is it correct to say that neo-liberal capitalism is in the interest of the developed countries?

## Conclusion

Neo-liberal Capitalism believes that free trade and free movement of capital along with everyone worshiping efficiency and profit would enrich all nations. Unfortunately this is not happening in the United States, the Mecca of Capitalism. In spite of a high per capita GDP, there is rampant inequality and poverty. The rich and the poor are moving farther and farther apart. Is it not astonishing that 38 million Americans live below the poverty line? Fifteen million children in the United States are growing up in poverty. Bill Gates fortune is equal to the net worth of 106 million poorest Americans or one-third of the US population. Is it the success or failure of Capitalism?

Neo-liberal Capitalism has not improved the lot of most of the people. It may have increased per capita GDP in some countries and created or enlarged an affluent middle class in many countries. But it has also increased income inequalities. It has not increased competition but led to hegemony of multinational corporations and dismantling of indigenous industries. People are encouraged and sometimes compelled to adapt to the needs of global corporations. For example, with the take over of Parle Industries by Coca Cola, Indians have no option but to drink foreign soft-drinks. We have a wide choice when buying computer hardware but have to go to Microsoft for the operating system. Governments that try to curb corporate excesses are accused of restraining of free market. The World Trade Organization faithful follows the role allotted to it by the developed nations to build free markets. It does not accept responsibility for the social, political and environmental cost of its decisions. Neo-liberal Capitalism was supposed to benefit everyone. That has not happened in the last 20 years. United States share of global trade has increased dramatically. The least developed countries including many African countries saw their share cut in half. The boats of the rich countries got bigger and more opulent. Those of the poor have been shrinking or sinking.

Whether we like it or not capitalism is in crisis. Capitalism as world religion upholds "Profit" as its God and relies on "Greed" as its sustaining faith. Its priests like bankers, brokers, economists, presidents, prime ministers, finance ministers glorify the virtues like competition and greed. But greed is self-destructive. It killed the goose that laid the golden egg. Greed almost killed the economies of the South East Asian countries, of Russia, of Brazil. Many more including the US are on the brink. If the economies of the developing world collapse one after the other, who will import from the developed world? South Korea's foreign exchange reserves grew from a few hundred millions dollars in 1997 to over 48 billion dollars in 1998, purely on reduction of imports. That represents 48 billion lost in exports by the developed world. Greed cannot sustain the world economy. Humanity, generosity and cooperation can. Let us hope and pray for a new global economic system that maximizes human happiness and brotherhood.

Karl Marx and Friedrich Engels had predicted that globalization of economy will precede the revolution and the global bourgeoisie will be their own grave diggers. This may be debatable. But one thing is clear for those who are unbiased, a system based on profit and greed, a system that is irreligious, that does not believe in human values, can never survive. A system that increases the gulf between the poor and the rich, between the privileged and the underprivileged, can never survive. The poor and the underprivileged will ensure that in the long run. Time is running out. We must change or perish.

# 15

# Communism

Communism is the very opposite of Capitalism. It was born out of the exploitation of the poor by the rich under the capitalist system. It was conceptualized by Karl Marx and Friedrich Engels in Germany in the 19th century in the form of the books *Das Capital* and the *Communist Manifesto*. It was brought into the world by Lenin through the Russian Revolution of 1917. It spread from the Soviet Union to other countries. Mao Tse Dzong adopted it with modifications in China. It spread to Eastern Europe after the Second World War. It was adopted by Fidel Castro in Cuba.

Communism was born out of idealism. It visualized a classless society where there were no rich or poor. It was based on the concept, "From each according to his ability, to each according to his needs." It sought to provide cradle to grave welfare. It sought to ensure that no one went hungry. Education was compulsory and free. So was health care. Children were the responsibility of the state and well cared for.

Communism denied the right to individuality. It denied the right to property, the right to freedom of individual choice, freedom of expression, freedom to worship and freedom to think. The State was supreme. The State owned all lands, all property, all means of production and all services. It decided who should be given what type of education, who would serve in what capacity. Central planning decided priorities for agriculture, infrastructure, development of science and technologies, rates of consumption and production and controlled the economy. The State controlled the lives of its people.

Communism did produce results. Soviet Union and China became world powers. Soviet Union beat America in putting the first satellite in space. Hundred per cent literacy was achieved. It did well in science and technology, in the fields of medicine, education, research and development. There were no slums. No one lived on less than one dollar per day. No one went hungry, but every thing was rationed.

Communism is a socio-economic structure that promotes the establishment of a classless, stateless society based on common ownership of the means of production. Its laudable ideal is "From each according to his ability and to each according to his needs." As the state of government owns all means of production, it also becomes responsible to meet every need of the people.

Communism as a political and socio-economic ideology had originated in Europe in the 19th century. After the Bolshevik Revolution of 1917, Soviet Union became the only sovereign communist country. By virtue of the Soviet Union's victory in the Second World War in 1945, the Soviet Army had occupied nations in both Eastern Europe and East Asia. As a result, communism as a movement spread to many new countries. This expansion of communism both in Europe and Asia gave rise to a few different branches such as Maoism. But they had a few common characteristics such as a single authoritarian ruling party, government ownership of all land and means of production a planned economy. The term planned economy means that the government will decide what kind and how much of goods and services the country will produce. The Eastern European countries which were forced into communism were Bulgaria, Czechoslovakia, East Germany, Poland, Hungary, Romania, Albania and Yugoslavia. In East Asia, China, North Korea and North Vietnam became communist. Cuba became a communist country after a revolution in 1959. Many countries in the developing world have communist parties. But they are not the rulers of any of the countries.

## Collapse of Communism

In 1985, Mikhail Gorbachev became leader of the Soviet Union and relaxed central control, in accordance with his reform policies of glasnost (openness) and perestroika (restructuring). The Soviet Union did not intervene as Poland, East Germany, Czechoslovakia, Bulgaria, Romania, and Hungary all abandoned Communist rule by 1990. In 1991, the Soviet Union itself dissolved. By the beginning of the 21st century, states controlled by Communist parties under a single-party system include the People's Republic of China, Cuba, Laos, North Korea and Vietnam. Communist parties, or their descendant parties, remain politically important in many countries.

Following the death of Mao Zedong in 1976, the People's Republic of China has reassessed many aspects of the Maoist legacy and the People's Republic of China. The People's Republic of China runs Special Economic Zones dedicated to market-oriented enterprise, free from central government control. Chinese successor of Mao Zedong, Deng Xiaoping accepted that a socialist country and the market economy model were not mutually exclusive. Officially, the leadership of the People's Republic of China refers to its policies as "Socialism with Chinese characteristics". Several other communist states have also attempted to implement market-based reforms, including Vietnam. The "third generation" of leadership under Jiang Zemin, Zhu Rongji, and associates largely continued Deng's progressive economic vision while overseeing the re-emergence of Chinese nationalism in the 1990s. As part of Jiang's nominal legacy, the CPC ratified the Three Represents into the 2003 revision of the Party Constitution as a "guiding ideology", encouraging the Party to represent "advanced productive forces, the progressive course of China's culture, and the fundamental interests of the people". There are various interpretations of the Three Represents. Most notably, the theory has legitimized the entry of private business owners and quasi-"bourgeoisie" elements into the party. The insistent road of focusing almost exclusively on economic growth has led to a wide range of serious social problems. The CPC's "fourth generation" of leadership under Hu Jintao and Wen Jiabao, after taking power in 2003, attempted reversing such a trend by bringing forth an integrated ideology that tackled both social and economic concerns. This new ideology was known as the creation of a Harmonious Society using the Scientific Development Concept. The degree of power the Party had on the state has gradually decreased as economic liberalizations progressed. The evolution of CCP ideology has gone through a number of defining changes that it no longer bears much resemblance to its founding principles. The CCP's current policies are fiercely rejected as capitalist by most communists, especially anti-revisionists, and by adherents of the Chinese New Left from within the PRC. Since the 1980s, as its commitment to Marxist ideology has appeared to wane, the party has begun to increasingly invoke Chinese nationalism as a legitimizing principle as opposed to the socialist construction for which the party was originally created.

Russia, Laos, Vietnam and, to a far lesser degree, Cuba have reduced state control of the economy in order to stimulate growth.

### Failure of Communism in the Soviet Union

Communism was against human nature. Human nature wants freedom. It wants freedom to choose, freedom to express himself, freedom to criticize. Since this was against the Communist doctrine, the state had to control the people. It required an authoritarian regime. It required isolation, the iron or bamboo curtain. It required mass indoctrination on the benefits of the communist society. It required control on consumption, control on thinking. It required the secret police to keep the population in control. Millions died. Communism had other problems. It killed individual initiative and enterprise. It bred inefficiencies. Production fell. There was acute shortage of consumer goods. The quality of life was not comparable to the developed West. In the classless society came a new class, the party functionary, the members of the politburo. There was nepotism. There was dissatisfaction. There was dissent. As world-wide communication improved, isolation became more and more difficult. The glimpses of the consumerism of the West was tantalizing. People craved for change.

## Transition to Free Market Economy

Communism has been discarded in the Soviet Union and in Eastern Europe. Western style free market has been adopted. But, to start with, the change was not beneficial to all, particularly in Russia and Romania. The change has pushed millions into abject poverty. Crime and prostitution has increased. Birth rates have fallen. Millions live below the poverty line. Millions of dreams have been shattered. Many now yearn for the old days of Communism when social security system ensured their honorable survival. But things are improving. As in China, Russia has adopted Nationalism and found a way to maintain a balance between welfare and economic growth, between state and private sectors and between planned growth and free market growth. East European countries are trying to integrate with the European economy. Vietnam, like Russia, has been able to practice Nationalism, establish economic ties with the US and become one of the fastest growing economies. North Korea is the only communist country which has failed to adapt to the situation arising out of collapse of the Soviet Union and can be called a failed state.

Cuba is perhaps the last and only surviving Communist country in the world. It embraced communism when Fidel Castro became prime minister in 1959. His revolutionary government nationalized all private property, public utilities, closed down the gambling industry and instituted tight controls on the private sector. Anti-Castro Cubans began to leave their country in great numbers and formed a burgeoning expatriate community in Miami that was opposed to the Castro government. The United States government became increasingly hostile towards the Castro-led government of Cuba. The fall of the Soviet Union in 1991 dealt Cuba a giant economic blow. The loss of the nearly five billion USD, that the Soviet government provided the Cuban government in aid in the form of a guaranteed export market for Cuban sugar and cheap oil, had a significant impact on the country's economy. Tightening of the embargo by the US Government was insufficient to persuade Cuba's Communists to surrender their grip on power. By the late 1990s, the situation in the country had stabilized. By then Cuba had more or less normal economic relations with most Latin American countries and had improved relations with the European Union, which began providing aid and loans to the island. Communist China also emerged as a new source of aid and support, even though Cuba had sided with the Soviets during the Sino-Soviet split of the 1960s. Cuba also found new allies in President Hugo Chávez of Venezuela and President Evo Morales of Bolivia, both major oil and gas exporters.

The Cuban government operates a much-lauded national health system and assumes full fiscal and administrative responsibility for the health care of its citizens. According to World Health Organization (WHO) statistics, life expectancy and infant mortality rates in Cuba have been comparable to Western industrialized countries since such information was first gathered in 1957. In 2007 according to UNICEF, Cuba and Canada have the lowest infant mortality rates in Americas followed by the USA. Many foreigners travel to Cuba for reliable and affordable health care.

The Cuban Government adheres to Communist principles in organizing its largely State controlled planned economy. Most of these means of production are owned and run by the government and most of the labor force is employed by the state. Recent years have seen a trend towards more private sector employment. By the year 2006, public sector employment was 78 per cent and the private sector at 22 per cent compared to the 1981 ratio of 91.8 per cent to 8.2 per cent. Like some other Communist and post-Communist states following the collapse of the Soviet Union, Cuba took limited free market-oriented measures to alleviate severe shortages of food, consumer goods, and services to make up for the ending of Soviet subsidies. These steps included allowing some self-employment in certain retail and light manufacturing sectors, the legalization of the use of the U.S. dollar in business, and the encouragement of tourism. In 1996 tourism surpassed the sugar industry as the largest source of hard currency for Cuba. The Cuban government has significantly developed its medical tourism capabilities as a key means to generate income for the country. Every year, thousands of European, Latin American, Canadian and American consumers with hard cash visit to access medical care services at up to 80 per cent less than U.S. costs. Venezuela's assistance of the Cuban economy comes chiefly through its supply of up to 80,000 barrels of oil per day in exchange for professional services and agricultural products. In the last decade, Cubans had received between US$ 600 million and US$ 1 billion annually, mostly from family members in the U.S. This number is influenced by the fact that U.S. government forbids its citizens to send more than $ 1,200 to Cuba to immediate family members, and then only once per year. In 2005 Cuba exported $ 2.4 billion, ranking 114 of 226 world countries, and imported $ 6.9 billion, ranking 87 of 226 countries. Its major trading partners include developed nations like the Netherlands, Canada, Spain, Italy, US and developing nations like China, Bermuda, Venezuela. Cuba's major exports are sugar, nickel, tobacco, fish, medical products, citrus, and coffee, imports include food, fuel, clothing, and machinery. Cuba presently holds debt in an amount estimated to be $ 13 billion, approximately 38 per cent of GDP. Cuba holds 6.4 per cent of the global market for nickel which constitutes about 25 per cent of total Cuban exports. Recently, large reserves of oil were found in the North Cuba Basin.

## Conclusion

Much to the chagrin of the Capitalist West, Communism has not been eradicated. It survives in China, North Korea and Cuba. China has been successful so far with its one nation two theory system. It has introduced controlled capitalism and consumerism in the coastal districts. It is keen to avoid the chaos which has gripped Russia. It is progressing slowly and cautiously with change.

Communism requires that the right to property be renounced. This is against human nature and particularly so for the rich and the influential. It can be ushered in only through revolution. Hence it is not an option that is available to most of the developing nations who believe in democracy to follow.

# 16

# Socialism

## Concept of Socialism

Socialism as an economic concept refers to a socio-economic system in which property and the distribution of wealth are subject to control by the government of the country. The modern socialist movement largely originated in the late-19th century Europe as a working class movement. Modern socialists like the Social Democrats in Germany or Labor Party in UK have carried out selective nationalization of key industries within the framework of mixed economies. Even the US had adopted a socio-economic system, the "New Deal", after the Great Depression of 1929 under President Roosevelt "The New Deal" had national health care, unemployment benefits and many other welfare measures not acceptable to neo-liberal capitalists.

Socialism may be described as a combination of Capitalism and Communism. It seeks to combine the best of the two extremes. It seeks to encourage individual enterprise and ingenuity. At the same time it seeks to provide cradle to grave welfare to its people. Profit is not its god and greed is not its religion. It seeks economic growth along with social justice, humanity, compassion and cooperation. In Socialism the Private Sector and the State Sector or Public Sector co-exist and complement each other. Economy is centrally planned and centrally controlled to a large extent. The market is not entirely free. Prices could be controlled through regulation on prices or through subsidies. Every effort is made to ensure that the rich poor divide is not allowed to go out of hand. But there are opportunities for individual enterprise and ingenuity to prosper.

## Socialism in Post-War Europe

The Social Democratic Party has been in power in Sweden since 1932. Labor parties also held power in Australia and New Zealand. After World War II, many socialist parties came to power in western Europe and implemented socialism. In 1945, the British Labor Party led by Clement Attlee was swept to power on a radical socialist program. Socialist parties also dominated post-war governments in France, Italy, Czechoslovakia, Belgium, Norway and other European countries. These governments nationalized major and economically vital industries while permitting a free market to continue in the rest. These were most often monopolistic or infrastructural industries like mail, railways, power and other utilities. In some instances a number of small, competing and often relatively poorly financed companies in the same sector were nationalized to form one government monopoly for the purpose of competent management or economic rescue. In the UK, the companies British Leyland and Rolls Royce fall in this category. This was achieved through compulsory purchase of the company with compensation. The nationalization of the coal mines in the UK in 1947 created a Coal Board charged with running the coal industry commercially. The social democratic governments in the post-war Europe thus introduced measures of social reform and wealth redistribution through state welfare and taxation policy. For instance the newly elected UK Labor government carried out nationalization of major utilities such as mines, gas, electricity, rail, iron and steel and the Bank of England. France claimed to be the most state controlled capitalist country in the world by carrying out many nationalizations. The Labor Party of Britain introduced National Health Service in 1945 bringing free health care to all for the first time. Social housing for working class families was provided in council housing estates and university education was made available for working class people through a grant system. Free school milk was introduced by Ellen Wilkinson, Minister for Education, in 1946. Generations of poor children grew up stronger and healthier because of this one small and inexpensive act of generosity by the Attlee government. In 1956, it is estimated that 25 per cent of industry was nationalized in the UK. However, the parliamentary leadership of the social democracies in general had no intention of ending capitalism. Their dedication to the maintenance of the post-war relationship with the US prevented the social democracies from moving to nationalize the multinational corporations or major industries of the countries. In fact most socialist parties of Europe rejected class struggle and Marxism and opted for mixed economy.

## Conflict with Neo-Liberal Capitalism

In 1980, with the rise of Republican President Ronald Regan in the U.S. and Conservative Prime Minister, Margaret Thatcher in Britain, the Western welfare states found themselves under increasing political pressure. Mrs. Thatcher had abolished free school milk for children when Education Secretary in the 1970-74 Conservative government. Neo-liberals attacked the social welfare systems in US and Britain as an impediment to individual entrepreneurship. Most welfare systems like health care was privatized in the two countries. West European socialists came under intense pressure to refashion their socio-economic policies in the late 1980s and early 1990s and to reconcile their traditional economic programs with the integration of a European Union based on liberalizing markets. The Labor Party in the United Kingdom went through a period of intense struggle between the socialist and liberal sections. By the 1990s, released from the pressure of the left, the British Labor Party, especially under the premiership of Tony Blair, put together a set of policies based on encouraging the market economy while promoting the involvement of private industry in delivering public services.

In 1989, the 18th Congress of the Socialist International at Stockholm adopted a "Declaration of Principles" which declares that "Democratic socialism is an international movement for freedom, social justice and solidarity. Its goal is to achieve a peaceful world where these basic values can be enhanced and where each individual can live a meaningful life with the full development of his or her personality and talents and with the guarantee of human and civil rights in a democratic framework of society." The objectives of the Party of European Socialists, the socialist bloc in the European Parliament, are "to pursue international aims in respect of the principles on which the European Union is based, namely principles of freedom, equality, solidarity, democracy, respect of Human Rights and Fundamental Freedoms, and respect for the Rule of Law." The rallying cry of the French Revolution—equality, liberty and fraternity—now constitute essential socialist values. The Russian socio-economic policies under President Putin can also be termed socialism.

## Socialism in the 21st Century

Socialism thus survives in Canada, the EU and Russia. It has re-emerged in recent times in some Latin American countries. Their champion is President Hugo Chávez of Venezuela. Chávez has an anti-imperialist and anti-US stance. He has rejected the policies of neo-liberalism and has carried part nationalization of oil production, land and other corporate assets in his country. The Bolivian President Evo Morales is a staunch ally of President Chávez. Brazil and Chile have also adopted socialism.

In the developing world, many parties and governments profess to be socialists. In China, the Chinese Communist Party has led a transition from the communist economy of the Mao period to an economic program they term the socialist market economy or "socialism with Chinese characteristics". Under Deng Xiaoping, the leadership of China embarked upon a program of market-based reform that was more sweeping than had been Soviet leader Mikhail Gorbachev's perestroika program of the late 1980s. Deng's program, however, maintained state ownership rights over land, state or cooperative ownership of much of the heavy industrial and manufacturing sectors and state influence in the banking and financial sectors. In South Africa the ANC abandoned its partial socialist allegiances on taking power and followed a standard neo-liberal route.

## Conclusion

Socialism is the goal of most of the developing countries. It is practiced successfully in much of Europe, particularly in Switzerland and the Scandinavian countries. There are parties with socialist ideology in Britain, France, Germany and many developing countries. It will be interesting to see whether socialism or capitalism will survive in the developed nations in the next century. Socialism has been extremely successful in most First World and Second World countries. This will be borne out by the economic and human development data given below:

| Country | Per Capita GDP PPP $ | HDI Ranking | % Population below Poverty Level |
|---|---|---|---|
| Canada | 35514 | 4 | 10.8 |
| Norway | 44648 | 2 | Negligible |
| France | 31825 | 10 | 6.2 |
| Switzerland | 38706 | 7 | Negligible |
| Sweden | 34735 | 6 | Negligible |
| Netherlands | 36937 | 9 | 10.5 |
| Russia | 12178 | 61 | 17.6 |
| Cuba | 4500 | 51 | Negligible |
| Chile | 12811 | 40 | 17 |

All these countries are classified as High in HDI rankings. The poverty level is as per the standards set by the country themselves and not 1 or 2 US $ per day. It will also be seen from the above list that Capitalist countries with socialist policies have very high per capita GDP which enables them to raise the resources required for welfare.

Socialism has not been too successful in the developing nations. These new born or young nations have not yet been able to master the art of governance. Feudal and vested interest are deep-set. Corruption is rampant. The countries, after years of colonization, are underdeveloped and poor. Per capita GDP is low. Infrastructure is inadequate. The resources available in terms of investable funds, natural and human resources are inadequate. Population growth is high and uncontrolled. Poverty is widespread. Education and health care are generally primitive. In simple terms, they are a century to half a century behind the developed nations in terms of development. Literacy is low. The ruling urban elite, irrespective of party affiliations, are engrossed in making their own lots better and at par with the consumerist West. Public sector is mostly managed by the bureaucracy with little incentive for profitability. It is inefficient, loss making, a drain on the countries limited resources and a barrier to progress. The voters lack political maturity. Political mandates are often fragmented and lead to ineffective governments.

The situation has been made worse by the pressures from the developed world, IMF, World Bank, WTO and internal vested interests to open up their economies, allow free market, free flow of foreign funds. Thus the "Cowboy Capitalism" or Neo-liberal Capitalism advocated by the Washington Consensus is the order of the day in most of the developing countries. The rich poor divide is widening. Political and social unrest is round the corner.

Socialism is a suitable socio-economic concept for the developing countries. It is followed successfully in some of the developed countries. But it is yet to be successfully implemented in any of the developing countries. The developing countries simply do not have the economic resources to throw out or nationalize the multinational corporations and implement socialism successfully.

# 17

# Concept of Nationalism

## Search for a Workable Economic Strategy

Communism has failed. Russia and China, the one time communist giants have moved away from Communism in search of economic survival. Communism has, more or less, disappeared from our world. In any case it can be ushered in only through revolution. The developing nations cannot afford revolutions. Hence developing countries cannot turn to Communism.

The most ardent supporters of Capitalism in the Western World admit that Capitalism is in crisis. Many economists are looking for a middle road between socialism and Neo-liberal Capitalism that is in fashion today. Writes John Oranto of Germany in a letter to the Editor of Newsweek, "Let us pray for continued enlightenment and a global economic system based on service,—one that maximizes human happiness rather than one that stimulates demands to consume or to collect." Gustavo Vinegra of Mexico wrote to the same periodical, "Socialism and Capitalism both have serious shortcomings. Real socialism (Communism) failed because it had sluggish responses to supply and demand. Now, real Capitalism (Neo-liberal Capitalism) is in crisis because its responses are too wide and fast. What about a new hybrid system?" Steve Bovingdon of Washington states, "The vision of globalization: Coke quaffing, Big Mac munching consumers everywhere driving their Toyotas and opening the latest Windows. This is a fundamentally flawed image for many reasons. First, this American style of development is gobbling up our natural resources and polluting what is left. Not only species are dying at an alarming rate, but whole languages and cultures are disappearing beneath sitcom reruns. Global Capitalism disproportionately benefits the wealthiest in the developing countries and further impoverishes the rest. While living in Central America, I saw the impact of "IMF structural adjustments". The landowners exported bananas more cheaply while the buying power of the workers wages plummeted. "Developing countries should work for self-sufficiency in food and feed their people." This is what Martha Hobart Burela of Spain has to say on Neo-liberal Capitalism. "It is encouraging that the United States is beginning to see that there are other approaches to 'good life' than those based solely on money, material goods and consumerism. Although the European Union has also jumped on the free market bandwagon and done much to rid itself of its state owned monopolies and otherwise condoned monopolistic practices, it is not buying the whole gung-ho package. We and the rest of the world still feel that giving free reign to the marketplace is brutal, that too many people will get trounced in the struggle. Not every one wants to make money the focus of their lives. The Capitalist idea is that the marketplace will, in the long run, balance out everything. But it is making the imbalance worse. The hawks of Capitalism must understand that there can be a middle road between cradle to grave welfare that has characterized so many European countries and the extreme of Cowboy Capitalism."

Socialism is certainly a model to follow. It is working well in Canada and many of the European countries. It also appears to be working in some countries like Venezuela and Russia where large groups are being lifted from below the poverty line. But socialism requires a very large government budget to implement the welfare measures. To implement the welfare measures, the government must have large revenues. This revenue can either come from a high rate of income tax as is prevalent in affluent countries like Canada and many of the countries of Europe. Or, the government must have large revenues from some source like crude oil in the case of Russia and Venezuela. Poor developing nations do not have the economic resources to implement socialism. They may also lack the political will to antagonize the domestic industries and multinational corporations by declaring their countries as a socialist state.

Is there a middle path between cradle to grave welfare and Neo-liberal capitalism as practiced by IMF, World Bank and WTO that can act as the economic policy for the developing nations? I believe there is. And that concept is NATIONALISM.

## What is Nationalism?

The Western world and the media have succeeded in portraying the word or concept of "nationalism" as a dirty word and an undesirable concept. To the Western world and the media, the word "NATIONALISM" conjures a vision of isolationism, jingoism, intolerance, reversal of economic reforms, anti-west attitudes and many other things. The reasons are not difficult to find. Western interests or interests of the multinational corporations and national interests of the developing world are not the same. The developed Western world primarily consisting of the United States, Europe and Japan today dominates the world economically and militarily. They have no desire to let go of this domination. Hence nationalism in the developing country is seen as a rebellion against this domination and is sought to be crushed in the same way as the demand of a serf or bonded labor for more freedom or justice from a landlord.

"Nationalism" is neither isolationism, nor jingoism, nor intolerance, nor reversal of economic reforms, nor anti-West. "Nationalism" is simply putting the interests of a nation and the majority of its people as its basic and core policy. "Nationalism" as a foreign policy seeks to protect the sovereignty of the nation and preserve its independence, both political and economic. It is enshrined in the UN Charter but conveniently ignored by the United States and Europe. The refusal of Yugoslavia to allow NATO forces on its soil to police the peace deal in Kosovo in the face of NATO bombing is one of the latest examples of political nationalism. The defiance of Iran in the face of bullying by the US and its allies to stop it from developing nuclear power is another example of Nationalism. "Nationalism" is the right to develop weapons and armed forces considered necessary to protect the country's territorial integrity. India's fundamental right to develop and test nuclear weapons and missiles is a manifestation of this policy.

"Nationalism" as an economic policy is to ensure that the economic policies are in the best interest of the nation and its people. It seeks to ensure that the country is not exploited by multinational corporations and economically stronger nations. It seeks to ensure social security and uplift the weaker sections of its society. It seeks to protect domestic industries, domestic agriculture, domestic employment and economic sovereignty to take economic decisions which it considers to be in its best interest.

Every developed country follows this policy. Japan does not permit import of cheap rice to protect its farmers. In spite of being a member of WTO, it has not fully opened its markets to the outside world. United States centrally controls agricultural production. It pays its farmers not to cultivate cultivable land so that over production does not lead to a drop in prices and make farming unproductive. Europe subsidizes its farmers to keep commodity prices like that of sugar competitive and ensure protection of its farmers against cheap imports. Only recently it imposed heavy duties on imports of tinned mushrooms from India, Indonesia and other developing countries. Even the world's largest economy, the United States, warns Japan to reduce export of steel to the United States because the domestic steel industry is adversely effected and some plants may have to close down leading to job losses. There are hundreds of examples of nationalist economic policies followed by the developed world.

United States itself is the world's number one practitioner of nationalism in all fields of its policy. The Hyde Act which requires the US president to certify that a country supports American foreign policy before it can be provided economic or military assistance is Nationalism. As a part of its national security policy, the US reserves the right to upgrade its nuclear weapon's technology and arsenal while denying similar rights to other nations. It wants Russia to scrap the Anti-Ballistic Missile

Treaty to enable it develop new anti-ballistic missiles and is using every pressure and inducement to get Russia to agree. It seeks to establish an anti-missile proliferation regime so that it can pound any country in the world with its cruise missiles, whenever it desires to do so, without the risk of retaliation. As a part of its nationalist foreign policy, it refuses to declare Pakistan a terrorist state and impose sanctions because the terrorism is directed against India and Afghanistan. But it has no problem in declaring Iran, Syria or Sudan terrorist states because the terrorism encouraged by these countries are directed against the Western world and its prodigy Israel. It had no qualms about getting President Allende of Chile murdered in a coup. It overthrew President Saddam Hussein of Iraq at the behest of Israel and the American Hawks. As a part of its nationalist economic policy, it supports globalization, opening up of markets, reduction of import duties by developing countries so that its multinationals can prosper. But it has no problem in restricting imports from developing countries through imposition of quotas, putting up non-trade barriers and using Resolution 301. It shamelessly forces IMF and World Bank to follow its dictates in matters of giving loans or imposing economic sanctions. It refuses to sign the Kyoto Protocol and refuses to reduce emission of green house gases to reduce global warming and climate change on the pretext that such measures will adversely effect US industry. The "Banana War" between United States and Europe is another example of American Nationalism. Europe gives preference to banana exporters from Africa and the Caribbean's over imports from Central and Latin America. Banana is produced in Central and Latin America by American multinationals. The European policy hurts the American multinationals and hence America. United States insists that Europe discards its policy in favor of the American multinationals. It has imposed punitive duties on some European products in retaliation. America is also not happy with Europe's negative attitude towards noisy American airplanes, its hormone enhanced beef and genetically modified food and has approached WTO to force Europe to accept these products. The protectionist lobby in the United States is pressurizing the US Government to retaliate against the European

Union on these accounts. It is not out of place to mention that British commentators are accusing the US administration as being in the pockets of the American multinationals who contribute generously to the campaign funds of US politicians. It is also acknowledged that the US has a long history of defending the banana company's interest in Latin America. To protect the assets of a plantation company in Latin America, the CIA, in 1954, helped to overthrow the then Socialist President of Guatemala. In early 90s, when an European Company tried to get into the central American market, its executives were chased away by armed police allegedly on the payroll of the American multinationals. Can we not follow the example of the United States, the only superpower of the world and practice "Nationalism".

### Why is Nationalism Necessary?

Interests of nations vary. For example, high crude oil prices benefit the countries which produce crude oil but are disastrous for countries which do not produce crude oil. Thus the Russian economy is growing at a rate of about 8 per cent while South Africa and Brazil are struggling to maintain a 5 per cent growth rate. India had a huge trade deficit of about 64 billion US $. But its current account deficit is only 18 billion US $, being reduced by inflow of remittances by millions of Indians working abroad, export of services, tourism and foreign investment. Thus, in spite of its trade deficit, its foreign exchange reserves are increasing each year and had reached almost 300 billion US $ by the end of 2007. Each nation is endowed with its own unique history, geography, culture, state of development and natural resources. Japan is one of world's largest producer of steel. It does not have any indigenous iron ore and imports its requirements mainly from India and Australia. Common sense tells us that it would be beneficial for India and Australia to produce the steel themselves instead of exporting iron ore. But that would not be in the interest of Japan.

Let us see some other examples. Japan favors a weak Yen because it helps exports. It has a trade surplus of over US $ 115 billion. United States on the other hand favors a strong dollar.

It is expected to have a $ 500 billion deficit in year 2007. A strong dollar helps to keep the cost of imports from developing countries low and contain inflation. The consumers in the United States benefit. Whenever the Yen tends to appreciate against the dollar due to the so-called market forces, the two governments get together to reverse the trend. Thus in the three-month period from December 1998 to February 1999, the Yen moved from 130 to a dollar to about 100 to a dollar and back to 120 to a dollar. A strong dollar is beneficial to the United States not only because it keeps the cost of imports down and thereby keeping inflation under control, it also makes foreign investment in the developing world cheaper and helps in its economic domination of the world. However, devaluation of a national currency of a developing nation against the dollar usually hurts their consumers, particularly its weaker sections, because essential imports of food, fuel and technology become costly. For example, in Indonesia, the people are paying three times what they were paying for a kilogram of rice in early 1997. Many cannot afford two meals per day.

Bank secrecy laws are beneficial to the developed nations. It helps the western banks in drawing billions of dollars from the third world and enriching themselves. Unscrupulous third world leaders like President Marcos of the Philippines, President Idi Amin of Kenya, President Mobutu of Congo to name a few have deposited billions of dollars in Swiss and other western banks. In 1999, the private banking services of the Citibank helped the brother of the deposed Mexican President to spirit away US $ 25 million out of the country. It is common knowledge that unscrupulous businessmen and corrupt politicians and government officials of many developing countries including India have stashed away billions of dollars of ill-gotten wealth in the developed world. Is it possible to have more information sharing about these accounts at Government to Government level? The answer is a simple no. The national interests of the developed and developing world are different. It is in the interest of the developed world to have dubious banks and banking practices, tax havens and banking secrecy laws which help them to siphon off hard currency from the developing nations without any effort or trade and make these developed countries economically stronger and the developing economies more vulnerable. It is the Western way of getting foreign investment from the developing countries free of cost.

Let us take the case of full convertibility. The developed world is pressing for the same. It induced Russia to opt for it. What was the result? An insatiable demand for dollars was created within the country itself leading to the collapse of the Russian Ruble and the Russian economy. If full convertibility was introduced into the Indian economy, every Indian with money to spare would be rushing to buy dollars. The entire foreign exchange reserves of the country could be wiped out in a matter of days and the Rupee will go the way of the Ruble. It is obvious that what is in the interest of the developed countries is not in the best interest of the developing world. China has a fixed conversion regime and capital controls. So has India except in the current account. But Malaysia's attempts to stabilize its currency through a conversion band regime and capital control measures is seen as a retrograde step and condemned by the World Bank, IMF and the US.

Let us take the case of low import duties. This is insisted upon by the developed world through the World Trade Organization (WTO). Low import duties make the cost of imported goods cheaper in the developing world and encourage their consumption. This increases the income of the developed world, reduces the income of the governments of the developing world and destroys the domestic industries. In the long run the industries of the developing world will be wiped out paving the way for total economic domination by the developed world. It will be obvious that the interests of the developed and developing world are different.

History has a very important role in the economic development of any country. It is no coincidence that all the developed nations have been independent nations for centuries. On the other hand most of the developing world gained their independence after the Second World War. Many of the developing countries have been colonized for centuries. Their wealth has been systematically taken away for hundreds of years and enriched the developed nations. The colonies were denied the right to develop indigenous technology. Raw material and minerals were taken away at throw away prices, value added and re-exported back to the colonies. That has been an important source of the finance for development and prosperity of the developed world. It is not reasonable to ask the developing world to compete with the developed world on equal terms. In any sport there are separate competitions for seniors and juniors. Developing countries are juniors in the economic field. They have every right to protect themselves from the seniors in the economic field, the developed nations. They have every right to demand level playing fields.

There is another connotation to the effect of history on economies. Israel was created by the Western world. Its development was financed by the developed world, mainly the United States and still is. The cold war helped in the development of Japan, Germany, Israel, Turkey, Pakistan, South Korea, Philippines and Taiwan as these countries received economic and military aid from the US in the name of containing Communism. These countries have gained tremendously from the economic and technological aid provided by the western nations. Japan and Germany were totally destroyed by the Second world war. Israel, Philippines and Taiwan are small countries with no natural resources whatsoever. On the other hand Cuba was isolated for being a communist country and Iran is being isolated for being anti-Israel. The developing world can thus be divided into the favored and the not favored by the US and its allies. It is only natural that those countries which are out of favor must find ways to protect their interests.

The state of literacy and development has an important bearing on economic policy. Developed nations do not need to spend much on education and health care. The infrastructure tor these services already exist. The governments of developing nations, on the other hand have to spend large sums of money on these aspects. The developed nations do not need to spend much on infrastructure. The infrastructure is already in place. In developing nations, infrastructure is a crying need. In developing nations, 25 to 35 per cent of the population lives below the poverty line. They cannot be allowed to starve to death. The developing nations, therefore, need subsidies and greater government spending.

Geography has an important bearing on the economies of countries. Russia with its inhospitable climate can never compete with countries with better climates in production of food grain. It has to import food to meet its needs. Australia and Canada on the other hand with vast land mass and minuscule population are surplus of food. How can the economic policies of such geographically different countries be the same?

Population and potential has a major effect on the economic policies of the developed world. China is an authoritarian communist country. But with its population over one billion it is seen as an emerging market. It has a record of human rights violations. Still the developed world is willing to do business with it on China's terms just to have access to this vast market. India, with its vast population and a million millionaires (persons with more than Rupees 25 million in assets), is also perceived as a major emerging market. But it is a democracy with corrupt politicians, corrupt government servants and unscrupulous businessmen. It is there to be exploited and is being exploited to the hilt. Bangladesh and Indonesia are also countries with vast population. But the countries have little potential as emerging markets and are generally neglected. So is Africa. Can such a diverse group of developing countries follow the same economic policies as desired by the developed world.

Natural resources also have an important bearing on the economies of the countries. Oil producing countries who earn in hard currencies find it easy to depend on imports. Countries like Bangladesh, India or Sri Lanka and many smaller Asian and African nations are incapable of earning foreign exchange to meet their essential import requirements. Small countries like Singapore and Hong Kong have no natural resources and are totally dependent on imports and trade for survival. Their assets are their location. Countries like Jordan and Palestine have nothing to export except labor. It is obvious that the import strategies of different countries have to be different.

Culture has also a role in the forming of economic policies. Corruption and crony capitalism is rampant in most of the developing world. There is, therefore, need for greater control on economic activities in these nations. There are greater need for monitoring and audit of government spending. Free market and total reliance on market forces can lead to unacceptable exploitation of the weaker sections of the society by the rich and the powerful and lead to social unrest. It is already happening in Indonesia. China has slowed down its reforms to guard against social unrest, caused by rising unemployment, from destabilizing the country.

The developed nations have different rules for themselves and the developing world. The IMF insists that loss making companies and banks in the developing world should not be bailed out by the Governments. Instead they should be offered for takeover by multinational banks and corporations. The IMF is unconcerned about the plight of the investors in these banks or companies or about the jobs lost. On the other hand the developing world welcomes the recapitalization of Japanese Banks by the Japanese Government. There is not a word of criticism of the United States for bailing out the hedge fund, Long Term Capital Management, which made over a billion dollar of loss in its investments or of bailing out countrywide, the largest mortgage fund of the US. No murmur has been heard about the British government recapitalization of the bank, Northern Rock which lost heavily in the US sub-prime mortgage collapse.

## Can Nationalism be Practiced?

Most affluent people in the developing world do not believe that nationalism can be practiced in the face of arm twisting by the developed world and their coercive economic tools, IMF, World Bank and WTO. Most of my countrymen, particularly the rich, the bureaucrats, the political leaders and the enlightened media, believe that we cannot survive as a nation without foreign investment, foreign goods and foreign loans. It is indeed difficult for our one million millionaires to live without starting the day with Kellogg's corn-flakes and listening to Good Morning India on a LCD Sony or LG television. It is below the dignity of our million millionaires to go to office on any thing less than a Mitsubishi Lancer or a Honda City or a Mercedes. It is unimaginable for them to wear a shirt not made by Van Husen or a T-Shirt not made by Lacoste or a shoe not made by Adidas or Rheabock or Tuffs. It is unimaginable to spend a day without drinking Coca Cola or Pepsi. What is life without eating a burger at McDonalds or Wimpys, having fried chicken at Kentucky Fried Chicken or a pizza at the Pizza Hut? It is unimaginable to kiss without taking Clarets, or make love without using an imported deodorant, perfume or condom. It is difficult to spend an evening without drinking Bacardi rum or Simrenhoff vodka or a decent imported scotch. What is the fun of having cancer smoking anything less than a 555 State Express or a Dunhill mild? Yes, without globalization and foreign investment, life would be dull and dreary for our million millionaires. How is money to be made if there is no foreign money. However, Nationalism will not hurt at least 800 million Indians who know nothing about these things. It will improve their lot.

China practices nationalism. It has joined WTO on its own terms. It accepts foreign investment but on its own terms, in areas where it considers it to be in its national interest to do so. It has its own perception of intellectual property rights and the patent regime. It has a fixed exchange rate and currency controls and is immune to the activities of currency speculators like George Soros, whose name sends chill down the spine of prime ministers and finance ministers of many developing countries. It may be argued that China is a vast country. It is the world's largest emerging market and second largest economy at PPP rates of GDP. It is a world military power. It can stand its ground in face of the developed world. Can we?

Malaysia practices nationalism. It is a small developing country. Its GDP (PPP) is 342 billion $ PPP compared to 4726 billion $ PPP of India. It practices a currency band conversion system after its currency was devalued as a part of the Asian meltdown. It has imposed capital controls and did not run to IMF for a bail out. It practices barter trade. A small developing nation like Malaysia can practice "Nationalism". Can we?

Cuba practices nationalism. It is a tiny country dominated and bullied by the United States with embargoes. It has suffered from economic sanctions placed on it by the United States for decades. It is not willing to change its national policies to get a few million dollars of foreign aid.

Iran practices nationalism. The sanctions imposed by the US and EU has effected its economy. But it does not believe that globalization and reforms, as recommended by the developed nations, is the only way out of economic difficulties.

Iran practices nationalism. It is pursuing its nuclear ambition in the face of a hostile US and its European allies, economic sanctions and betrayal by some turncoat friends like India.

Yugoslavia practices nationalism. It is a tiny mountainous country with hardly any natural resources. But it had the spirit to stand up to the might of United States and NATO. It was being bombed day and night. Its cities, industries and infrastructure were being systematically destroyed. There were casualties. But they were undaunted. They were not willing to compromise on political or economic sovereignty. It is a different matter that a little over half the population has been weaned away from their nationalist stand by Europe. Whether they will gain or loose, only time will tell.

It is my firm conviction that all developing nations can practice nationalism. It is in their long-term interest to do so. But it calls for a determined leadership. It calls for sacrifices in the short-term. It calls for living without or with less Coca Cola, with less foreign goods, reduced consumption and slower growth rates. It is not going to be easy. The developed nations are ganged up against it and will try every trick from economic arm twisting, to spending billions of dollars on media propaganda, lobbying and buying influence. They will spend billions of dollars to create political instability and to put in place a regime of their choice. The privileged in the country are against it and will do their best to further their own interests.

The people of the developing countries must decide whether they want to be birds in a gilded cage with goodies served to them on a plate or they want to be free but willing to face the challenges of the wild. They must wonder if they fought long battles for independence only to become economic slaves of the developed world. They must choose between the "Neo-liberal Capitalism" devised for them by the Washington Consensus among the IMF, World Bank, the US treasury and their creation the WTO to enslave the developing world and "Nationalism", their only hope of survival.

Sadruddin Aga Khan, President of the Bellerive Foundation, writes in his article, 'Free Market Failures', "Providing a better system requires three things: We must slow down the rate at which we cede sovereignty to the global marketplace: We must build checks and balances into existing international economic instruments, with greater public participation and investor responsibility: and we must strengthen the parallel system of checks and balances found in the UN system of institutions. These are complicated problems demanding many difficult decisions, but surely it is wiser to trust in our ability to solve them intelligently and democratically rather than put our faith in a free-trade panacea that is dismally flawed."

## Fundamentals of Economic Nationalism

*The first fundamental step is to get rid of hot money or foreign investment in domestic stock markets.* Hot money has been identified as the real culprit behind triggering the collapse of the South East Asian currencies and economies in 1997-98. The funds look nice on the foreign exchange reserves and a healthy reserve gives the feeling of invincibility of the Titanic. Like the unsinkability of the Titanic, it is not a reality but a feeling created in the minds of the people through systematic propaganda, by hard sell. In reality it is sitting on an economic time bomb which can go off any moment. 17 billion US $ worth of foreign investment entered the Indian stock market in 2007 and raised the BSE Index from about 11000 to 21000 points. The repatriation of US dollars by foreign investors in the wake of the sub-prime crisis in the US brought the BSE Index below 9000 and hurt millions of retail investors while the foreign investors walked away with their profits. Can any investor dare to imagine if another 4 billion US $ leaves the Indian market at this point in time. The result will be total economic disaster. Developing countries must try to ease hot money out with increased taxation, greater regulation and other economic means. If that does not seem feasible, get the domestic mutual funds to start selling first. That way the Foreign Financial Institutions will make less profits and the damage will be bearable. The move will not make the domestic investors, mutual funds and brokers happy. But their happiness is less important than national economic security. If we are not ready to take such a drastic measure, at the very least put in place currency controls like what Malaysia has done. At least you will be able to ensure that the country cannot be ruined as you sleep.

*The second fundamental step is get out of WTO or at least scuttle the Doha Round of negotiations.* WTO was devised by the developed world to prize open domestic markets in the developing world and allow exports of capital, goods and services from the developed world and their all powerful multinationals. The rules are totally loaded in favor of the rich countries of the world. Forget the hard sell. Like the products in any advertisement, the product generally promises much and delivers little. Just like Hindustan Lever's Wheel detergent does not have any lime as advertised but only a little essence of lime, WTO's charter of free trade is a one way street. It means free exports from the developed world to the developing world and restricted exports from the developing world to the developed world. Added to that will be take over of all indigenous manufacturing and services including banking and insurance which require very little investment, has very little risk and lots of profit and economic power. If you do not believe me, ask the Indian garment exporters and the stainless steel exporters to Europe, the tinned mushroom exporters from India and Indonesia and the lighting equipment exporters from Australia and New Zealand. Mr. Vajpayee, the ex Indian Prime Minister lamented on this phenomena in his address to the G 15 meeting in the Caribbean. The sooner the leaders of the developing countries realize this, the better off their countries will be. Mr. Kamal Nath, the Indian Commerce Minister, along with his counterparts in the G 26 nations have done a remarkable job in protecting the interest of the developing countries. There is nothing to be afraid of. Russia is not a member of WTO. It does not stop the G 7 countries from trading with it. Taiwan and Vietnam are not members of WTO. It does not prevent the US from investing in them or trading with them. The G 7 countries need our markets. They cannot survive without it. And they understand their interests far more clearly than we do. They will trade with the any developing country, whether they are members of WTO or not, as long as it is in their interest to do so. Where profit is the God and greed is the sustaining religion, Western companies will sell whatever they can, wherever they can and whenever they can as long as they make profit. Is it not true that Western companies sold arms, missile technology and components, nuclear technology and components to Iraq and Pakistan? Is it not true that the US Senate is worried about sale of state of the art weapons technologies to China by US companies.

*The third fundamental step is to legislate your own patent regime.* Unless this is done, it is only a matter of time before all traditional domestic products, industrial, medicinal and agricultural, will be patented by the Americans and sold back to the country at a hefty margin or royalties charged. Things are getting out of hand. There is not time to be lost.

## Developing a Nationalist Economic Policy

The first step in forming a Nationalist economic policy is to carry out a SWOT analysis of the nations' economic strengths, weaknesses, opportunities and threats. To ensure objectivity during the analysis, it is necessary to keep the vested interests out of it. This is easier said than done.

Having done the SWOT analysis, the next step would be to set achievable economic goals. The danger here is that necessity to achieve short-term political goals may result in the sacrifice of the long-term economic and political goals of the country. It is hoped that the political leaders of the country would have sufficient statesmanship and vision to avoid this. The temptation of achieving a growth rate that is not sustainable has to be guarded against. One of the reasons for the collapse of the Asian Tigers in 1987-88 was that the targeted growth rates were unsustainable.

They were due to the inflow of hundreds of billions of dollars of foreign investment which resulted in surplus capacities. The export targets were too high. The capacities generated were too much. There was too much foreign investment and debt. It required one little tremor to bring down the house of cards.

Having done the SWOT analysis and set the economic goals, it is necessary to examine the different ways of achieving them. For example, if one of the economic objectives is to reduce the trade deficit, it can be achieved by increasing exports as India is unsuccessfully trying to do or to reduce imports as South Korea has successfully done. These different options have to be carefully examined in light of the decision criteria which could include expected economic benefits, expected social costs, expected political fallouts, possible effect on the currency and exchange rates, possible effect on balance of payment position and foreign investment. This should include a sensitivity analysis which should cater for the following eventualities in the environment:

- Hardening of world recessionary trends and difficulties in achieving export targets.
- Flight of hot money and possible effect on currency.
- Drying up of foreign investment.
- Reduced agricultural output due to unfavorable weather or natural calamities.
- Increase in the world oil prices.

The next step would be to prepare the action plan necessary to achieve the selected economic objectives. This plan would primarily consist of the following:

- Formulation of the budget proposals.
- Identifying needs for special legislation and the possibility of getting these passed.
- Executive action like negotiation and signing of trade treaties with trading partners on bilateral or regional basis.

## Conclusion

It is considered that national economic policies in the developing world are unduly influenced by the views of the IMF, World Bank, the United States Treasury and the WTO and the domestic vested interests. Unless the developing countries understand the threat they face from Neo-liberal Capitalism, they will soon be swallowed up by the economic superpowers, loose their economic and political sovereignty and revert back to the colonial era. General Electric's have purchased assets worth 1 billion US $ for just 500 million in South East Asia. Unless something drastic happens, it is only a matter of time before all the tools of production in the developing world would be owned by the multinational corporations of the developed world.

Nationalism is the only means of survival for the developing world. It is a different matter that the actions of the multinational corporations are not in the interest of the developed world either. The slowdown in the US economy bears testimony to that. But that would be the subject of a different book.

# PART III

# IMPLEMENTATION OF NATIONALISM

# 18

# A Swot Analysis on India

## Some Fact About India

India has a population of 1.1 billion which is growing at a rate of 1.4 per cent. By the end of 2007, India has emerged as the fourth largest economy in the world with a GDP PPP of 5.15 trillion \$. In Rupee terms it amounts to 200 trillion. India is the largest producer in the world of milk, cashew nuts, coconuts, tea, ginger, turmeric and black pepper. It also has the world's largest cattle population (193 million). It is the second largest producer of wheat, rice, sugar, groundnut and inland fish. It is the third largest producer of tobacco. India accounts for 10 per cent of the world fruit production with first rank in the production of banana. India is 14th in the world in factory output. Manufacturing sector, in addition to mining, quarrying, electricity and gas, together accounts for 27.6 per cent of the GDP and employs 17 per cent of the total workforce. Economic reforms introduced after 1991 brought foreign competition, led to privatization of certain public sector industries, opened up sectors hitherto reserved for the public sector and led to an expansion in the production of fast-moving consumer goods. The telecom industry is one of the fastest growing industries in India. India has nearly 200 million telephone lines making it the third largest network in the world after China and USA. With a growth rate of 45 per cent, Indian telecom industry has the highest growth rate in the world. Thirty-four Indian companies have been listed in the Forbes Global 2000 ranking for 2007.

India had about 5.6 billion barrels of proven oil reserves as of January 2007, which is the second-largest amount in the Asia-Pacific region behind China. On the negative side, the per capita income PPP is 4726 $, which is less than countries like Brazil, Thailand, Malaysia and places it in low income countries as per World Bank classification. It is ranked 165 out of 185 countries in the Human Development Index.

## Land of Contradictions

India is a country of extremes and contradictions. Geographically, we have the highest and longest mountain ranges, the Himalayas as also one of the longest sea coastline. We have tropical jungles and deserts. We have the hottest and coldest regions of the world in Churu in Rajasthan and Dras or Siachin in Kashmir. We have cities like Mumbai, Delhi, Chennai, Kolkata, Bangalore and Hyderabad which can compare with the biggest in the world. On the other hand we have villages which are not accessible except on foot. We have villages which have no electricity, no water supply and no modern day sanitation. We produce 200 million tons of food grain and yet starvation deaths are reported occasionally from some states. We produce Nobel Prize winners in literature, science and economics. Foreign students from Africa and the Middle East come to study in our universities. Yet 400 million Indians are illiterate. We have some of the best hospitals in the developing world and attract medical tourists from the developed world. Yet about 800 million Indians are without basic health care, safe drinking water and toilets. We have jeans or suit clad men and miniskirt or designer clothes wearing women in the cities and men and women wearing nothing but loin cloth in some of our remote tribal areas. Culturally we have coke drinking, big Mac munching, disco dancing young men and women in the cities, enjoying free sex and imbibing the MTV ushered westernized culture. In the rural areas we have child marriages, caste systems and total ban on free mixing. Four Indians are in the top ten of Forbes list of billionaires. We have one million millionaires (persons whose personal assets are more than 40 million of Indian rupees). We have 34 per cent of our population or about 350 million people living below the poverty line.

India is an enigma. It has enormous potential but deplorable performance. There is a difference of a century or even ten centuries of development between its modern cities and its remote villages. It is an elitist society where development is of the rich, by the rich and for the rich. Its focus of development is the major urban areas. In its sixty years of independence, little attention has been given to the development of rural areas and remote villages. Free market reforms are not going to change that. What Ms. Tavleen Singh observes is true. Poverty was there even before reforms started. But fifteen years of reforms have not reduced poverty. It has only increased the disparities. India needs to evolve an economic approach to development and growth that narrows down differences and not widens them. It needs effective government spending in areas like education, health care and rural and infrastructure development.

## Swot Analysis

### *Strengths*

The main strengths of the Indian Economy are as under:

*Size*. The Indian economy is large with a gross national product (PPP) of over 5.15 trillion \$. It has a population of over 1.1 billion. It has the world's largest middle class and over one million millionaires. It is one of the largest emerging markets. Its policies and practices may not be liked by the developed world, particularly United States. But no country can ignore it.

*Natural Resources*. India has been endowed with vast natural resources in the form of minerals, biodiversity and climate. Except for gold, copper and tin, it has most of the other minerals. It has crude oil. But the quantities are not enough to meet its internal needs. It has almost unlimited reserves of poor quality coal and almost unlimited potential for generating hydro-electric power.

*Technological Development.* India is the most technologically developed country in the developing world. It can produce anything from satellites, rockets, aircraft, railway equipment, cars, super computers, every type of consumer durables and electronic equipment. The Indian workforce has proved adept at technology absorption and can operate in the most sophisticated technological environment. This is true even in rural areas where not only are tractors and other farm equipment successfully maintained but an improvised motor vehicle called the "Jugar" costing less than US $ 1000 has been developed and operated. In this aspect it is a leader in the developing world. It is a world hub for Information Technology and Business Process Outsourcing.

*Self-sufficiency in Food Production.* India produced more than 200 million tonnes of food grain in 1998-99. It has replaced the United States as the largest producer of milk in the world. India is self-sufficient in food production except for pulses and edible oil. This is in spite of much of its cultivable land being without irrigation and the per hectare yield being almost half of that obtaining in the developed world. With better irrigation, farming technology and seeds, it has the potential to become a major producer and exporter of food.

*Technical Manpower.* India is one of the largest exporters of technical manpower. Its software professionals are as good as any in the world. Adequate trained manpower is available in all technical and professional skills.

*Well Developed Financial Institutions.* India has well developed financial institutions like banks, mutual funds, insurance companies, stock markets and business institutions. It has sound economic laws and an independent and fair judicial system.

*Domestic Saving Rate.* The domestic saving rate is high. The figures in the last three budgets indicate this. If this saving can be effectively utilized, much can be achieved.

## Weaknesses

India has a number of weaknesses which prevent it from fulfilling its potential of becoming a world economic power. Some of these are:

*Timidity*. Most Indians including the Government are timid. They do not seem to realize or appreciate their strengths and potential. Be it cricket, hockey, or politics, the spirit to do or die, to fight to the finish is non-existent. Unlike the Afghans or the Serbs who could never be subdued by any foreign power, India has been ruled by rulers of foreign origin for more than the last ten centuries. Leaders like Rana Pratap or Shivaji who considered independence more important than peace and comfort were few and far between. Indians are essentially traders and natural neo-liberal capitalists. "Money" has been their god and "greed" their sustaining religion for centuries. Sacrifice and nationalism are so uncommon that any one who sacrifices himself for a cause is considered to be a fool or a hero. "Compromise and survive" has been the national ethos for centuries. Indian leaders are easily cowed down by threat or influenced by inducements. They tested the atom bomb and immediately became apologetic about it and agreed to sign the CTBT as soon as a face saving situation can be created. The Americans could ban 50 Indian companies but India could not ban one American company in retaliation. There was too many dollars to be lost. The rich Indians cannot bear hardship and privation. Hence Indians are poor bargainers.

*Weak Governments*. Most Indian governments are weak, ideologically confused and unable to take unpopular but essential decisions. They appear afraid of the United States, IMF, World Bank and WTO and are incapable of protecting national interests. In this respect they could learn much from the way China deals with the United States and its western allies. Some examples of this are handing over the seed business to foreign companies, allowing the American multinational to carry out experiments with genetically modified seeds, inability to protect national interest in the patenting of traditional Indian biodiversity, medicine and Basmati rice by American companies, allowing unrestricted import of foreign goods and opening up the insurance sector. Europe does not accept genetically altered seeds or genetically modified food stuff. A British court ordered Mosanto to pay thousands of dollars in damages caused to farmers for not taking adequate precautions during field experiments. Many of the Ministers lack competence, vision and professional integrity. They easily succumb to pressures from vested interests both within and outside the country. There is a marked lack of in-depth analysis and objectivity in decision-making. The bureaucracy is negative in its approach and play games with impunity to get their way. There is a marked lack of accountability for incorrect decisions taken.

*Corruption.* Corruption has been one of the pervasive problems affecting India. It takes the form of bribes, evasion of tax and exchange controls, embezzlement, etc. From birth to death a person has to bribe to get anything. Be it getting a birth certificate, school admission, college admission, getting a ration card, getting a job, posting or transfer, a telephone connection, water connection, electricity connection, gas connection, a train reservation, passport, bank loan and other clearances for setting up a business, to getting a death certificate, if you want it within a reasonable period of time, you must have connections, political influence or simply pay the required bribe. If you have done something wrong like committed a traffic offense or even some serious crime like rape or murder, the chances are 90 to 10 of your being able to get away scot free if you can bribe the police or have the right political connections. You can totally avoid or substantially reduce payment of all kinds of government dues like income tax, sales tax, exercise duty, customs duty, octroi duty, house tax, property tax and so on if you know the right people and are willing to share the savings with the authorities concerned. The corruption in recruitment in government departments is shameful and most demoralizing for the youth. In Assam, one has to pay Rs. 50,000 to become a primary school teacher. In Rajasthan, one has to pay a hefty sum of Rs. 60,000 for the lowly job of "Gram Sevak" or village assistant. Whether it is central government departments like railways, armed forces, customs, etc. or state government departments like PWD, irrigation, police, primary and secondary school teachers, etc., most jobs come with a price tag. Payments have also to be made by government servants for postings, transfers, allocation of accommodation, etc. The more lucrative (read with more chances of earning money through bribes), the higher the sum required to be paid. It is a difficult environment for one to work honestly.

The economic reforms of 1991 reduced the red tape, bureaucracy and the Licence Raj that had strangled private enterprise and was blamed for the corruption and inefficiencies. Yet, a 2005 study by Transparency International India found that more than half of those surveyed had first-hand experience of paying a bribe or peddling influence to get a job done in a public office. The chief economic consequences of corruption are the loss to the exchequer, an unhealthy climate for investment and an increase in the cost of government-subsidized services. The Transparency International's India study estimates the monetary value of petty corruption in 11 basic services provided by the government, like education, healthcare, judiciary, police, etc., to be around Rs. 2.1 billion. India still ranks in the bottom quartile of developing nations in terms of the ease of doing business, and compared with China, the average time taken to secure the clearances for a start-up or to invoke bankruptcy is much greater. The Right to Information Act (2005) and equivalent acts in the states that require government officials to furnish information requested by citizens or face punitive action, computerization of services and various central and state government acts that established vigilance commissions have considerably reduced corruption or at least have opened up avenues to redress grievances. The 2006 report by Transparency International puts India at 70th place and states that significant improvements were made by India in reducing corruption.

*Environmental Degradation.* About 1.2 billion people in developing nations lack clean, safe water because most household and industrial wastes are dumped directly into rivers and lakes without treatment. This contributes to the rapid increase in waterborne diseases in humans. As per World Health Organization report for 1992, out of India's 3119 towns and cities, just 209 have partial treatment facilities, and only 8 have full wastewater treatment facilities. 114 cities dump untreated sewage and partially cremated bodies directly into the Ganges river. Downstream, the untreated water is used for drinking, bathing and washing. This situation is typical of many rivers in India as well as other developing countries. Globally, but especially in developing nations like India where people cook with fuel wood and coal over open fires, about 4 billion humans suffer continuous exposure to smoke.

*Poor Tax Compliance*. Indian has over 100 million middle class. Only about 20 million of them pay taxes. Tax evasion is a national pastime with almost every one indulging in it. This is the major reason for the poor state of finances of the Central and State Governments. Due to vested interests, government after government is simply unwilling to tackle this menace. The reluctance to tax agricultural income is difficult to understand. Farmers have paid one-fourth of their produce as tax from the time of Ashoka till the time the British left in 1947. But they are not required to pay tax now. A clerk who earns Rs. 150,000 as salary has to pay tax but a landlord who earns Rs. 300,000 a year producing grapes, strawberries or sugar cane does not pay income tax. Is there any justification for such discrimination?

*Lack of Nationalism*. Indians have little or no national pride. Their nationalism starts and ends with celebrating a victory of the Indian cricket team. Most Indians and particularly the affluent have a great fascination for foreign culture, foreign goods and foreign travel. This is not a new phenomena. It is a legacy from the British days when the WOGs or Westernized Oriental Gentlemen ruled the roost. Even government secretaries, who are reasonably honest, can be influenced by being looked after abroad. The Indian elite cannot consider themselves elite if they cannot drink foreign whiskey, use foreign cars, use other foreign goods, jump ques, commit traffic offenses and other crimes and get away with it without any punishment. Air India offers Hineken Beer and Grants scotch whiskey instead of offering Kingfisher Beer and Peter Scot, Antiquity or Single Malt whiskey which are just as good. The Indira Gandhi international airport terminal building leaks profusely whenever it rains, but we do not have the pride to repair it. Hence we are never able to act in national interest.

*Lack of Professionalism in Business*. Most of the Indian companies lack professionalism in their dealings. Making a fast buck is their only motive. There is a lack of quality control and commitment to fulfil contracts or commitments at all cost. There is no commitment to upgrading technologies or doing research and development. For most, foreign collaboration is the easy way out. Under invoicing of exports and over invoicing of imports and stashing foreign exchange abroad is a national pastime. So is making money through influence peddling and exploiting loophole in law or through the simple process of bribing concerned government officials. The penalties are too less and the legal process too long to effectively curb these practices.

*Poor Work Culture and Labor Unrest.* Most Indian workers, particularly the government servants, believe in earning maximum emoluments with minimum productivity. There is no sense of responsibility or concern for the public. There is no work ethics. There is no discipline. If I ever go to my local branch of the State Bank of India at 10 A.M. the time for opening the counters, the only persons to be found in the bank are the manager, the assistant manager, the peons and the watchman. No transaction can be done before 10.30 A.M. at the very earliest. The managers seem totally incapable of taking any action against anyone. The unions have become a law unto themselves and hold the country to ransom with all kinds of unreasonable demands. India has the highest number of public holidays in the world. Bandhs, work to rule, strikes in the Governments and public sector units cause enormous economic losses and inconvenience to the public at large. Government departments are reported to be 30 per cent over staffed. But reducing the staff in face of agitation is not possible. Unless labor can be tamed, the economic future of the country is bleak. Twenty-five per cent of Government School teachers do not attend school but get their salaries.

*Infrastructure.* In spite of the developments in the last ten years, the lack of infrastructure continues to be a major bottleneck to development. The transportation systems like roads, railways and ports are congested. Power is another major problem. So is water supply. Whatever infrastructure does exist is generally poorly maintained. The government departments responsible are too busy obtaining money from contractors to supervise effectively. No senior officer leaves his air-conditioned office to see the state of affairs for himself. Tours are generally treated as paid holidays. There is no accountability at the senior level.

*Farming Technology and Infrastructure.* Sixty-six per cent Indians work on farms and produce 33 per cent of the GDP. Almost 500 millions are engaged in this activity. But 60 per cent of them are illiterate. Ninety-five per cent of them have no formal training in agriculture. The result is low productivity. The farming infrastructure is poor. High quality seeds are not available in many areas. Credit is a problem. Credit cards have been introduced, but the numbers covered are not even 1 per cent of the total farmers. A good harvest is often a curse rather than a boon. In the absence of proper storage and marketing facilities, prices crash. There have been years where potato prices crashed to an extent that the farmers did not find it worthwhile even to harvest the crop.

### Opportunities

The US economy is on the brink of a recession. In spite of this, the environment presents many opportunities which need to be seized with energetic and detailed action plans. Some of these are:

*Markets in the Developing Countries.* India is the most technically and industrially developed amongst the developing world. It can produce world class products. It can compete, price-wise, with the products of the developed world and export railway equipment, various kinds of machines, consumer durables, electronic and electrical equipment and a host of other products. But we export very little to the developing world. In our obsession with trading with the developed world, we have neglected this trade. Shortage of foreign exchange in the trading partner can be overcome through balanced trade. This will help to remove the recessionary tendencies and generate employment.

*Non Dollar Trade.* The availability of foreign exchange restricts the purchasing power of the developing countries. If the requirement of foreign exchange could be removed or reduced from bilateral trade, the volume of trade could grow dramatically. As India is by far the largest developing country (China excluding), it is only logical that we should take the lead in this direction. Non dollar trade can take two forms, barter trade or local currency trade. Barter trade has been practiced from time immemorial. Local currency or Rupee trade has been practiced between India and the Soviet Union. This type of trade has enormous potential, particularly in border areas. It only requires the will, the initiative and ingenuity.

*Oil Exporting Countries*. The boom in oil prices has resulted in all oil producing countries being flush with hard currencies. Every effort needs to be made to increase trade with these countries through exports of goods and services like development of infrastructure, industries, real estate and information technology. Setting up educational institutions and health care facilities could also be tried.

*Domestic Market*. The domestic market in India is large enough to attract the multinationals in every segment of our economy. The Indian economy can achieve a healthy economic growth if it can generate demand by empowering its weaker sections of the society, particularly the farmers in the rural areas. The per capita GDP of the rural areas is less than one-third of that of the urban areas. To increase the per capita GDP of the rural areas, it has to be ensured that the farmers get remunerative price for their produce. It is the middle men, the traders who seem to get the most benefits from rising food prices. If the multinationals could be eased out, the market is large enough to sustain Indian industries and achieve a healthy growth. Says Mr. Mukesh Ambani, Chairman Dhirubhai Mukesh Ambani Reliance Industries, "We have to act now and act decisively, build on our domestic industry and guard against recession."

### Threats

The primary threats to the Indian economy are as under:

*Increasing Imports*. India has liberalized its import policy to include all kinds non-essential foreign products like cosmetics, cereals, liquor, cigarettes, garments, consumer durables, electronic equipment, soft drinks, confectionery and so on. These imports are bound to result in a serious drain on our foreign exchange reserves. Indian exports have been growing but imports have been growing faster. Thus we have a trade deficit of about

$ 62 billion in 2006-07 up from $ 7 billion in 1998-99. Inflows from export of IT services and remittances from Indians working abroad have helped to improve current account balance. Foreign exchange reserves also appear adequate. But things can change quickly. The rising crude oil prices and slow down in the global economy could reduce exports and increase value of imports and establish a negative trend. We need to be watchful.

*Cheap Imports.* Cheap imports in key sectors like steel, coal, fertilizer, synthetic fiber can kill these core industries. The numbers of dumping cases are on the rise. Cheap imports of cotton and edible oil can cause untold misery to the domestic farmers. Cheap imports, particularly from China, are capturing our markets at the cost of domestic industries. The Government seems powerless to do anything about it. It is interesting to note that the developed nations, who operate under the same WTO regime, do not allow such activities. Japan does not allow import of rice to protect its farmers. Europe does not allow cheap import of stainless steel from India. Americans have imposed heavy duties on Indian exports of tinned mushrooms. America has warned Japan against excessive export of cheap steel.

*Trade Deficit.* Increasing imports and decreasing exports has made the current account balance precarious. The trade deficit is steadily increasing and touched US $ 62 billion in 2007. This will in turn increase our dependence on foreign investments and loans to get foreign exchange to cover the trade deficit. Excessive foreign exchange debt and foreign exchange investment will make the country vulnerable and could lead to total dependence on the developed world for our economic survival.

*Rise in Oil Prices.* Oil prices in the world were at all time high of over $ 140 per barrel. The price has fallen below $ 50 US but a depreciating Rupee has cancelled some of the gains. The oil import bill is rising. The government has not passed the price increase to the consumer fully. But this will increase budget deficit and ruin domestic oil companies. There will be inflation and the requirement of foreign exchange for oil imports will increase. There is always a danger of any crisis blowing up into a full-fledged war and disrupting of oil supplies. The only viable solution is to appreciate the rupee to match the increase in oil prices so that the Rupee cost of the oil imports remain the same.

*Collapse of the Rupee.* The Rupee had strengthened somewhat against the US dollar but not against the British Pound or Euro. The foreign funds collected in the form of Global Depository Receipts are due for redemption in foreign currency. Billions of dollars invested in stock markets may be withdrawn at any time. This will create additional demand for foreign exchange. The export lobby will demand devaluation. All this will create pressure on the Rupee. As likely as not, the government will succumb to the pressure and devalue the currency. This could bruise investor confidence and lead to a flight of money. The Rupee will, therefore, go into a free fall like the South East Asian currencies did in 1997. Cost of imports will rise. Cost of import of gold and oil will rise. Hyper inflation would hit the country.

*Debt Trap.* The governments revenues are not keeping pace with the growth in Governments expenditure due to more than generous increases in emoluments to Government servants in the Sixth Pay Commission and populist measures like Employment Guarantee Scheme and loan waivers to farmers. The total debt of the government has doubled from 3,14,000 crores in 1990-91 to 7,73,541 crores in 1997-98. Government borrowings have increased from about 35,000 crores in 1991-92 to over 100,000 crores in 1998-99. The interest payments have grown from about 25,000 crores to 80,000 crores in the corresponding period. Thus out of every rupee borrowed, 94 paise goes to pay interest on old debt. The states have an additional debt of 200,000 crores and the amount is increasing every year. How can the country survive if the money borrowed does not generate profits to pay back the loan taken. We are on the verge of collapse. The solution recommended by many is disinvestment of shares in the Public sector companies. This is ridiculous. One does not get rich by selling performing assets. The government must reduce non-productive expenditure and generate more income.

*Social Unrest.* It is naive to expect that the Indian poor, the farmers, the slum dwellers, the unemployed youth will silently suffer and perish. Unless the nation can take effective steps to reduce the rich poor divide and make it possible for all its citizen, to earn two square meals a day, there will be increasing crime and social unrest. The signs are already visible. Trafficking in women and prostitution is on the rise. Cases of kidnapping for ransom, murder for profit and extortion are increasing. More and more youth are indulging in it. The cover story of *India Today*, January 18, 1999 is frightening. Says Delhi Police Chief, Mr. V.N. Singh, "93 per cent of all the heinous crimes of this year has been committed by young novices". Murder, robbery and extortion are occurring daily in our cities. Youth in the age group from 16 to 30 were responsible for 69 per cent rapes, 66 per cent kidnappings, 63 per cent robberies and 55 per cent attempted murders. Unless effective steps are taken to limit consumerism and reduce unemployment, each one of us will be paying protection money to the local unemployed youth (read anti-socials) every month for our very survival. We used to hear of Western kids killing for a pair of trendy sneakers or money to buy ice-cream. Such events have started happening in our cities like Mumbai and Delhi.

*Acquisition of Indian Industry by Multinationals.* Successful Indian private sector companies and weak public sector companies become takeover targets for multinationals. Such takeovers, particularly hostile takeovers, are not in the interest of the nation. Domestic industry must be protected. The nation can never prosper by disinvesting its profit making public sector units and by handing over its profitable private sector companies to multinationals. Nobody wants to acquire a loss making company except at bargain prices. In such cases the buyer is the gainer and the country is the looser. Disinvestment of shares of profitable public sector companies is a retrograde step. The Government should give these companies more autonomy and let them function like private companies.

*Compulsive Populism.* India is democracy where 60 per cent of its voters are illiterate and have very little understanding of what is good for them in the long run. All the political parties try to woo these voters with sops like free electricity, free water supply and writing off of loans. Encroachment of government land is condoned and even encouraged. Water and electricity is provided free of cost to the encroachers. Labor cannot be disciplined and productivity cannot be demanded. Economically desirable actions like closing down loss making factories and industries is not carried out. People are not penalized for non-payment of taxes or evasion of duties. Thousands of millions of funds which could be invested in development projects, which generate income and employment, are thus frittered away. The Indian politicians and political parties can give away anything that belongs to the government if they feel that this will improve their prospects at the elections. The central and the state governments together spent 940 billion on non-merit subsidies. Subsidies on water and sanitation were 32 billion. Subsidies on water charges for irrigation were 1200 billion. The subsidies by state electricity boards amounted to 96 billion. Unless this tendency can be curbed, the economy of the country can never improve. Unfortunately, the free bees do not always help masses. To reduce expenditure on free supply and theft of electricity, the power supplied to consumers is reduced through power cuts. To contain the expenditure or subsidizing cooking gas, the supply has been capped. The rich pay double the price in the black market, the dealers laugh all the way to the bank and the ordinary consumer does not get his gas when it finishes.

## Conclusion

The strengths and weaknesses of the developing countries will differ. But the opportunities and threats remain more or less similar. The SWOT analysis should be the first step in deciding the economic objectives of the nation.

# 19

# Economic Objectives and Analysis of Options

The SWOT analysis carried out in the previous chapter, to my mind, gives rise to a number of economic objectives. The list is illustrative rather than exhaustive. These are discussed in the succeeding paragraphs.

## Analysis of Options

### *Keep the Rupee Strong*

To have a strong Rupee, the availability of Foreign Exchange must exceed requirements. This can be achieved through two methods. One is through manipulation of market forces. The other is by introducing a fixed exchange regime. Let us examine each of them.

*Defense Through Manipulation of Market Forces.* This approach requires that the availability of dollars exceeds demand. Foreign exchange is received in different ways. These are:

*Foreign Investment in the Share Market.* This is the "hot money" that has been the cause of world's economic instability. The less we have this type of foreign investment, the better off and more stable will our economy be. To reduce this type of foreign exchange inflows we can increase the tax or adopt other regulatory measures. However, the domestic investors will not like it as Foreign Institutional Investors (FIIs) boost markets and boost returns in the short run.

*Foreign Direct Investment.* Foreign direct investment can be beneficial to the country as long as it does not create surplus capacities and net foreign exchange outflows. It should also not result in unfair competition with domestic industries. Foreign investment should not be permitted in consumer industries unless there is a commitment to export.

*Export Earnings*. This is one of the major sources of foreign exchange. However, as we have seen already in the chapter on "Feasibility of Export Oriented Growth", prospects of increasing this form of earning through exports to the developed world does not exist in view of the slow down of the economies in the developed world.

*Remittances by NRIs and Indians Working Abroad*. This is an important source of non-refundable foreign exchange. It is a major contributor to balancing our current account and our foreign exchange reserves. There is a need to provide an incentive to get these remittances through official channels. A simple one is to give them a 5 per cent higher conversion rate if the funds are remitted through Indian banks.

*Foreign Investments in Indian Government Bonds and Banks*. The India Resurgent Bonds, Global Depository Receipts and NRI deposits in banks are examples. These are not earnings but amount to loans and have to be returned with interest at the agreed time. These help to tide over the short-term problems but are potential long-term problems if they are not productively used to earn foreign exchange.

*Market Borrowing*. This is foreign exchange borrowed from commercial banks abroad by the government of India, Indian companies and subsidiaries of multinationals in India. These are potentially hazardous unless these loans can generate the foreign exchange required to repay the loan. This was one of the reasons for collapse of the Asian Tiger Economies. This type of borrowing requires strict monitoring. Unfortunately, IMF and WTO do not permit it.

*Tourism*. Foreign tourists coming to India are an important source of non-refundable foreign exchange. The NRIs and Indians working abroad visiting India fall in the same category. This is a very desirable type of foreign exchange. If we concentrated on improving our tourism infrastructure and made it more tourist friendly, we could not only earn a lot more foreign exchange but also generate employment. It is sad that small countries like Singapore and Thailand attract four times the number of tourists who visit India.

*Loans from IMF, ADB, World Bank.* These are low interest long-term loans which are very useful for developing countries. These loans are welcome as long as they do not come with conditions which impinge on the economic sovereignty of the country.

*Export of Services.* Export of Information Technology and Business Process Outsourcing services have proved to be major foreign exchange earners.

Manipulation of such a diverse set of market forces is extremely difficult if not impossible. Foreign exchange reserves, even if very big, do not ensure a strong and stable currency. Japan has over US $ 900 billion of Foreign Exchange Reserve and a trade surplus of US $ 117.3 billion. Yet it has a weak yen and violent fluctuations in its exchange rate.

*Defense of the Rupee Through Legislation.* As we have seen above, the Rupee cannot be defended by manipulation of market forces. In 1997, Hong Kong spent over 30 billion dollars to defend its currency. India cannot afford to do so. Other countries such as Thailand, South Korea, Malaysia and Brazil also failed and lost precious foreign exchange in the bargain. If market forces are allowed free play, the Rupee can be brought to its knee any time if the foreign financial institutions consider it in their interest to do so. As soon as rupee begins to weaken, exporters do not bring in the foreign exchange earned in the hope of making profit. This creates shortage of foreign exchange and weakens the Rupee further. On the other hand, when the Rupee is strengthening, the exporters are in a hurry to repatriate the foreign exchange to avoid loss. This increases availability of foreign exchange and further strengthens the Rupee.

The only way to defend the Rupee is to fix its conversion rate through legislation. To start with, it can be fixed at its present level. It may be a good idea to appreciate the rupee gradually at a rate of half rupee per quarter. This will force exporters to repatriate the foreign exchange earned quickly and not hold it back in the hope that the rupee will depreciate and they will make some additional profit. It will also progressively reduce the cost of essential imports.

### Get Out of WTO

WTO membership conditions amount to an unequal treaty. It is heavily loaded in favor of the developed nations. It is imperative that India gets out of WTO. Continued membership can result in the economic takeover of the Indian economy by the Western Economic powers, their multinational corporations and investors. Continued membership can lead to closing down the small scale industries and the handloom sectors or open them to competition from foreign products. This will increase unemployment and poverty. If India is to survive and be free to take decisions which are in its national interest, it must get out of WTO. Sooner this is done the better. This aspect has been discussed in detail in the chapter titled "WTO and the Developing Countries". However, the Indian Government is unlikely to get out of WTO. The Indian nationalists will have to takeover. Enough social unrest will have to be created so that the so-called foreign investor confidence evaporates in spite of the best efforts of the Governments. The multinationals will have to be chased away through the path of agitation. The world must never feel that the so-called economic reforms, namely globalization and privatization, can never be rolled back. The threat of another Indira Gandhi coming and nationalizing private industries and throwing out the multinationals must remain for ever.

### Declare War on Corruption

If there is one reason why, in spite of all its advantages, India has failed to fulfil its potential to be a world economic and military power, it is its all pervasive corruption. A legacy form the colonial days, it is increasing rather than decreasing. Rajiv Gandhi, former Indian Prime Minister, once lamented that only 10 per cent of funds earmarked for development ever reached the target population. The rest went to line the pockets of the politicians, bureaucrats, government servants responsible for overseeing the execution of the project and the contractors executing the project. Mr. Rahul Gandhi, son of Rajiv Gandhi says that things have worsened and only 5 per cent of funds intended for development reach the target population. If we want our economy back on rails, me must deal with corruption. There are three options to deal with corruption.

*Computerize and Improve Procedures.* Computerization can reduce corruption. We have seen this happen in railway bookings. However, it has not been able to eliminate it all together. One can still get one's name up the ladder on payment of a suitable consideration to the touts. But computerization certainly helps as it speeds up recovery of information and is most suitable for giving programmed decisions. Computerizing records like those of births, deaths, land records, calculation of taxes could certainly help in minimizing corruption. Improving procedures certainly helps. Laying down that a contractor's bill, once submitted, must be paid within 48 hours has helped in cutting down corruption. Laying down time limits for activities in government departments and their strict monitoring would go a long way in reducing corruption. However, any system is as good or as bad as the people who implement them. Good, honest leadership and reduction in political interference will certainly help matters.

*Hunt Down the Corrupt and Weed Them Out.* It is time government stopped turning a blind eye to the corruption in government departments and took effective action to throw out the corrupt government servants. Punishment has never stopped crime. But, it is also true, more effective the law and order machinery, lesser is the crime. Similarly, more effective the vigilance system and certainty of deterrent punishment, less will be the corruption.

*Make Possession of Large Quantities of Cash an Offense.* Cash is the source and end product of all forms of corruption. The gains from corruption and tax evasion are generally held in sack-full or carton-full or locker full of cash. This cash goes out of circulation and cannot be productively used. If holding of cash beyond one hundred thousand is made an offence, excess possession of cash will be eliminated. This will reduce money available for paying bribes. The receivers of the bribe will also find it difficult to keep the money and would continuously spend sleepless nights over it. It will also be easier to hunt down the corrupt and quickly seize the ill gotten wealth.

### *Reduce Imports*

If the Indian economy is to be saved from collapse, we must import only essential items. Some ways of doing it are:

*Raise Import Duties*. This is simple enough to implement if we could get out of the WTO. If the import costs are high, imports will automatically drop. Some will argue that high import duties will encourage smuggling. So be it. If the import duties are low and no smuggling is expected, why not disband the Customs and the coast guard. Let them perform their duties and catch the smugglers. In any case the elimination of gold smuggling has not been an unqualified success. With their traditional source of income gone, the smugglers have taken to extortion. Of the two types of crimes, smuggling seems to be more acceptable.

*Make Import Procedures Complicated*. The open general license system should be abolished. Every import should require a sanction. It can be ensured that bureaucratic delays are increased instead of being decreased. The fees for processing such applications can also be increased and made proportional to the value of the imports. This will definitely reduce imports.

*Social Agitation*. Social agitation on the lines of the "Swadeshi Andolan" (Nationalist Agitation) launched by Mahatma Gandhi in the pre-independence days can be launched again. Effort can be made to educate masses on which products and brands are imported and require to be boycotted and what is not. It is unbelievable but true that most Indians cannot distinguish between Indian and foreign products. One wonders what Swadeshi Jagaran Manch has been doing all these years. We occasionally hear their name but never see their activities except occasional destruction of some soft-drink bottles. Shops stocking imported goods can also be boycotted. People using imported goods can also be socially boycotted. A threat of physical harm may work.

### Reduce Consumption of Petroleum Products

*Popularize Battery Powered Vehicles.* Battery powered vehicles do not consume petroleum products and do not produce carbon dioxide. I have purchased a Hero Honda Electric model called Maxima. It costs about Rs. 30,000 or $ 750. It costs half a Rupee or about 1 US cent per km to run. If the millions of students who use two-wheeler switched to this type of vehicle, import of crude oil could be reduced substantially. Battery powered cars are also available but are not given adequate publicity. Governments of developing countries should promote the use of these vehicles by subsidizing their cost instead of subsidizing cost of petroleum products.

*Strengthen Public Transport Systems.* Efficient public transport systems like Metro Rail System, local train services, bus, minibus, shared taxis will reduce the number of vehicles on the road, consumption of petroleum products and pollution.

*Increase Taxes on Private Cars.* Increasing excise duty, registration fee and other taxes will increase the cost of cars and hopefully reduce their sale. Even if it doesn't, the additional so revenue generated will come in handy for subsidizing battery powered vehicles and public transport.

### Sustain Economic Growth

India has achieved excellent growth in the last decade. This growth rate must be maintained to eliminate poverty. Some possible methods are discussed below:

*Increase Government Spending.* Increase in Government expenditure in planned development, particularly in infrastructure such as surface transport, electricity, minor irrigation and water harvesting has always benefited the economy and stimulated economic growth. It is, therefore, desirable to increase government expenditure on plan projects.

*Start Barter and Balanced Trade in Real Earnest.* A large number of developing countries have requirements of goods and services but do not have the foreign exchange to buy them. India with its large range of high quality products in automotive, electronics, consumer durables, garments, food processing industries have much to offer to these countries. In return we could import equal value or barter products like raw cashew, cotton, edible oil, pulses, metals and minerals. Other products which are offered but not required in India could be re-exported.

*Start Local Currency Trade.* Local currency trade implies that we allow countries who buy Indian products to pay fully or partly in their own currencies. This will make it easier for us to export our products and compete effectively with western and Chinese exports. For example if we offer a truck on 75 per cent payment in hard currency and the rest in their local currency, it is likely that most developing countries would accept it. The local currencies so earned can be used by the industries for meeting transportation, marketing costs and after sale service establishments, new joint venture companies, etc. Whatever will be surplus with the company will be taken over by the Government of India who will convert the currency at an agreed rate into Indian Rupees and hand it over to the company. The local currency so earned by the Government can be used by them purchase of goods and services from that country, for meeting expenses of the embassy or high commissions, financing of trade delegations, tourism, payment of airport and port charges, etc. The balance if any could be given to other companies for setting up business in that country or used to provide foreign aid. The system is akin to the PL 480 food aid given by America to India in the early 'sixties. This measure has great potential to boost our industrial production, increase GDP and employment. It could also be used in our border areas by having currency exchange counters at local post offices.

### Improve Availability of Foreign Exchange

There are various options to boost foreign exchange earnings. Some of the important ones are given below:

*Increase Exports.* This is the most popular method. However, it is unlikely to succeed because the economies of the world's most developed countries are slowing down. Their demands for imports are also falling. There is rising protectionism in these countries. The range of exportable products to the developed world is limited and low value. Even if the volumes do marginally increase the result would be marginal.

*Reduce Imports.* This aspect has been discussed earlier in detail.

*Give Incentive to Expatriate Indians and Foreigners to Remit Funds.* The expatriate Indians and foreigners studying or living in India, and foreign charities are an important source of non-refundable foreign exchange. It will help if the "Hawala" or unauthorized foreign exchange dealers are eliminated by giving the expatriate Indians 5 per cent more rupees than the authorized conversion rate, if they send their money through Indian Banks. This incentive will not be available to loans or investments in stocks markets. Other incentives can be thought of. The key criteria for incentives are that the foreign exchange sent has to be converted to Rupees and spent in India.

*Strengthen the Rupee.* Controlled appreciation of Rupee will encourage exporters to remit foreign exchange rather than trying to hold it or sell it abroad.

*Discourage Foreign Travel for Non-productive Purposes.* This can be done by imposing a foreign travel tax and charging a 5 per cent service tax for foreign currency drawn for tourist travel abroad.

*Make Improving Tourism a Key Result Area.* Foreign tourists are a good source of foreign exchange. Our tourism infrastructure is woefully inadequate. It is not so much a matter of the number of hotel rooms or welcoming with garlands. What is lacking is tourist friendliness and hospitality. There is a need to improve security of the tourists and to ensure they are not cheated and exploited. The Indian approach to a foreign tourist is that here is a person to be exploited. The attitude is self-defeating. My brother settled in the United States complains that Indian Hotels charge him more room rent for the same room as compared to an Indian customer. If anything, a person paying in dollars should be charged less. It is this exploitive attitude which turns off the tourist. Tourist information services must improve and be manned by friendly staff. Complaints of exploitation must be immediately attended to. Special police stations must be set up at important tourist centers. Traders, hoteliers, taxi drivers cheating foreign tourists must be given exemplary punishment. It is the standard of service which attracts tourist to destinations like Singapore.

### *Increase Government Revenue*

The Government needs large amounts of funds to improve infrastructure and carry out rural development. The Government income can be increased by the following measures:

*Tax Agricultural Income.* The farmers have paid a fourth of their produce as tax from time immemorial. They have had a tax holiday for 50 years. If a clerk earning Rs. 6000 per month as salary can pay tax, why shouldn't a landlord earning Rs. 300,000 per year from cultivation of grapes, strawberries or sugarcane pay taxes. Why should money of the urban taxpayer be used to develop the rural infrastructure? The holy cows must be eliminated. Every one must contribute to national development. If elected governments cannot introduce taxation of agricultural income for political considerations, let us declare economic emergency and have president's rule for six months.

*Improve Tax Compliance.* There is far too much of tax evasion in the country. This needs to be ruthlessly curbed. The revenue intelligence system needs to be improved and all persons liable to pay tax must pay tax.

*Sustain Economic Growth.* The economy is growing at a healthy rate and the collections from indirect taxes have increased. However, the budget deficit is still large. Economic growth needs to be sustained.

*Close Down or Rehabilitate the Loss Making Public Sector Units.* The loss making Public Sector Units cost the Government over Rs. 200 billion per year. This is totally unacceptable as these are a burden on every single Indian. Whereas "profit" is not our god and "greed" is not our religion, "inefficiency and loss" are our devil and has to be exorcised. Rs. 17 billion were earmarked for payment of salaries of sick Public Sector Units. These loss making behemoths should either be modernized and made profitable or they should be closed. If some jobs are lost, it is regrettable but unavoidable. In the interest of the nation a few have to suffer. Genuine efforts need to be made to rehabilitate the retrenched workers. Some of these companies may be handed over to the unions to run for one or two years if they seem capable. All government enterprises must be cost effective and profitable. If it is not, it must be closed or privatized.

### Reduce Government Debt

The government is close to a debt trap. Government borrowing has crossed Rs. one trillion per year. Eighty per cent of it goes repaying interest. Government borrowing must be reduced and brought under control. This can be done by increasing government revenue and decreasing non-plan expenditure.

### Protect Domestic Industries

*Protect Indian Companies.* The WTO puts multinationals at par with local companies and expects the local companies to compete with the multinationals on equal terms. This is ridiculous. The multinationals with their multi billion dollar capital base can absorb a loss of billions of dollars in a year without batting an eyelid. McDonalds have operated in India for about 12 years before making a profit. Ninety per cent indigenous companies will be totally wiped out if they made a loss of $ 500 million. One does not put a fly weight boxer to box with a heavy weight in the same ring. That would be grossly unfair.

*Protect Traditional Small Scale Industries.* Traditional industries like handlooms, powerlooms, cane, bamboo items provide employment to millions of people in rural areas and small cities. Competition from foreign and indigenous industries could kill these industries and push millions into abject poverty. These industries must be protected and strengthened. Their designs must be protected by law from mass reproduction in alternate material like plastics by law.

*Erect Trade Barriers.* The developed world imposes quotas for export of garments and other products to the countries of the developing world. Then there are protectionist subsidies and anti-dumping duties. When trade barriers fail to serve the requirements of protectionism in the developed countries, they fall back on non trade barriers. There is US resolution 301, ban on use of child labor, fishing without using turtle proof nets, hygiene standards and so on. Finally there is economic sanction and black listing of companies for political disagreements of the local government with governments of developed countries. Fighting these barriers are costly and time consuming. The developing world just cannot afford it. They must not suffer silently in the face other forms of arm twisting. They must learn to retaliate with their own import quotas and non trade barriers.

### *Ensure Remunerative Prices to Farmers*

Food security and self-sufficiency is vital for the country. More than 65 per cent of the population or about 650 million people are dependent on farming for sustenance. They are the poorest section of our society. The national demand for goods and services cannot show much improvement unless the purchasing power of the farmers can be increased. To make this possible the farmers must get remunerative prices for their produce. This can be done through the following measures:

*Lay Down Remunerative Procurement Prices.* We need to lay down minimum procurement prices for not only grains but also to staple vegetables like potato and onions and fruits.

*Organize Effective Countrywide Procurement.* Unless there is effective procurement, laying down minimum prices have no meaning at all. Whereas procurement is effective in some states like Punjab and Haryana, it is practically non-existent in states like Assam. It is understandable that Food Corporation of India cannot set up establishments in remote areas unless adequate volumes are available. One way to overcome this problem is to train and finance unemployed youth of these remote areas to get into this business. They should act as sub-agents and procure food stuff from "hats" or weekly rural market places and deliver the products to regional storage center. Market yards must be established at each "tehsil" or subdivision.

*Increase storage facilities for grains and cold storages for storage of perishables.* This should also be opened to private sector and bank finances provided for capacity generation. This is another area where educated unemployed rural youth can be assisted to participate through technical and financial assistance.

*Encourage formation of marketing co-operatives like Amul.* The marketing support available to the farmers is woefully inadequate. In the absence of this support the farmers are exploited by moneylenders and traders. The marketing support for agricultural products must receive the highest priority.

### *Concentrate on Rural Development*

Eight hundred million of our population live in small towns and rural areas. Unless employment opportunities, education, health care and recreation facilities increase in the rural areas, the migration of population will continue from the rural areas to the cities. Our cities are collapsing under the weight of this migration. Basic amenities like electric power, water supply, sewage disposal cannot be provided. Slums are springing up everyday creating sub-human living environments. This immigration has to stop. This can be done by the following measures:

*Encouraging NGOs to Participate in Rural Development.* The Government must encouraging NGOs to participate in development of village infrastructure by reimbursing cost of completed projects or involving them in project implementation. This system has worked extremely well in Earthquake Rehabilitation Project in Maharashtra. It is a model worth giving a try.

*Organize Consultancy Support.* Providing competent consultants at District Collector level to expedite project formulation and estimates will expedite project sanctioning. Decentralizing development planning at the "panchayat level" or village level makes sense in establishment of priorities. But the technical expertise for project formulation, execution and supervision available at the village level is totally inadequate. "Panchayats" or village councils must identify the projects. But planning and execution must remain in the hands of competent and committed experts.

*Training and Financing Self-Employment in Rural Areas.* It is essential to train and finance rural educated unemployed to get into the business of procurement, storage, preservation, processing and marketing of food stuff. Poultry, fishery and animal husbandry needs to be encouraged. This is one possible way of increasing rural employment. This should be made a key result area.

*Involve the Local Population in Execution and Maintenance.* This is very important. It has been repeatedly seen that involvement of Tribals help in successful aforestation. The local population has the maximum stake in rural development. They must participate in its construction and maintenance. It generates income of the local people. However, the operation and maintenance must be adequately supervised so that the benefits of the development are not usurped by a few and vested interests do not distort the projects.

*Abolish Child Labor.* There are more children under the age of 14 in India than the entire population of the US. The great challenge of India is to provide sufficient nutrition, education and health care to these children. Children under 14 constitute nearly 3.6 per cent of the total labor force in the country. Nine out of every ten of these children work in their own rural family settings. Around 85 per cent of them are engaged in traditional agricultural activities. Less than 9 per cent work in manufacturing, services and repairs. Child labor is a complex problem that is basically rooted in poverty. The Indian government is implementing the world's largest child labor elimination program, with primary education targeted for 250 million children. Numerous non-governmental and voluntary organizations are also involved. Special investigation cells have been set up in states to enforce existing laws banning employment of children (under 14) in hazardous industries. The allocation of the Government of India for the eradication of child labor was $ 10 million in

1995-96 and $ 16 million in 1996-97. The allocation for 2007 is $ 21 million.

### *Protect Indian Biodiversity*

With the opening up of our economy under the WTO regime, our biodiversity is under attack from multinational companies. There were attempts to patent Neem and Turmeric Products by American companies. This was fought off with great difficulties. Now Basmati rice used in India for centuries has been patented by an American Company. This patent has to be contested in foreign courts. All that cost valuable foreign exchange and the outcome is never certain. There are many other medicinal plant genes which are being stolen or patented by foreign companies. Unless the government can stop this piracy, our traditional products will be patented by foreign companies and sold to us at exorbitant prices. Our patent laws need to be redefined and patenting products available in the Indian biodiversity and ancient sciences like "Ayurveda" contested by the government at every level.

### *Protect Indian Industry and Agriculture*

Indian industry and agriculture are also under threat. Under the WTO regime, import duties are being constantly reduced. Cheap imports of many products like fertilizers, steel, coal, synthetic fiber, cotton, tea, coffee, rubber are swamping the Indian market. This could result in the destruction of our Industry and agriculture. This must be stopped.

### *Taming the Labor Unions and Increasing Productivity*

The Indian Labor Unions, particularly the Central and State Government Unions have become a law unto themselves. They are not averse to bringing the Nation to a standstill to get their demands, justifiable or otherwise, conceded by the Government. The Government also has the habit of starting on a tough note and then conceding the demands in the face of agitation. This has encouraged the Unions to toughen their stand on agitating and blackmailing the Government. This has to be stopped. The policy of appeasement must end. The Unions must be tamed. Labor disputes must be settled in Labor Courts and other courts. The agitational approach must be stopped for ever. The Government's dealing with the ATC strike was effective though the tough measures could have been taken earlier and saved hundreds of millions of Rupees of economic loss. There should be a fight to finish at the next strike. Some actions that must be taken are:

*Promulgate a Law Declaring All Strikes by Essential Services and Government Servants Illegal.* We need to declare strikes by these elements illegal and dismiss the leaders forthwith and take them into custody. We need to paralyze the lives of the strikers and their families by cutting off water and power supply of the dwellings of the workers. The colonies of the striking government employees must be placed under curfew to stop them or their families from moving out of their house. People who disrupt the lives of the whole nation cannot be allowed to enjoy paid holidays without having their lives disrupted. We need to ensure that the striking workers lose seniority and their pay for days spent on strike is forfeited. There should be no condoning the offense at the end of the strike. Persons indulging in any form of violence must be arrested, charge-sheeted and face trial. They must be imprisoned if found guilty. Government employees not participating in the strike must be given protection and rewarded.

*Good Leadership is Required to Improve Productivity.* Good leadership is necessary for motivation of the working staff. Officers must be positive, result oriented and consumer friendly. The work to rule attitude must disappear. There must be periodic training of officers in management and attitude. Ineffective officers must be sidelined and never given independent charge. The necessity of productivity must be explained to the workers. Every worker must produce more than his salary and perks. A method of measuring productivity must be laid down and achievements of individuals must be evaluated every six months. Consistent under performers must be dismissed at the pleasure of the President. The attitude that a government servant cannot be dismissed and performance is not important must disappear. Discipline must be maintained at the workplace. Late coming, irregular attendance and impolite behavior must not be tolerated. Workers must receive work related and attitudinal training. Self-pride in competence and the organization must be created. The basic attitude has to be "Service Before Self". The Government servant must serve the population. Black sheep and bad examples must be weeded out. The service regulations in the Government departments must be amended to provide for dismissal on grounds of neglect of duties or customer apathy.

*Decentralization of Decision-Making in Government Offices and Public Sector Units is a must.* The attitude that all people are corrupt and hence financial control has to be centralized is wrong and outdated. When my daughter joined Citibank as an assistant manager, her discretionary powers were US $ 1000 or over Rs. 30,000. As a senior Army Officer with 20 years, I never had such discretionary powers. Thus things move too slowly. In the government, urgently needed equipment or spares cannot be procured in time because of centralization of economic powers. Thus efficiency suffers. But it does not prevent misappropriation. The scams in Bihar and other governments bear testimony to that. What is required to be ensured is that authority and responsibility go together. It must also be ensured that negligence, lack of application of mind and dishonesty does not go unpunished.

Let us see an example of effect of leadership on a government organization. In 1970, the Damodar Valley Corporation, DVC for short, was a Public Sector Undertaking that generated power in Bihar. Like some other poorly run Public Sector Units, DVC was generating at only about 50 per cent of installed capacity and was a loss making concern. In 1972 it was taken over by a retired Army General called P.S. Bhagat. During his first inspection of one of the power plants, he noticed that one of the units was not functioning. When asked why, he was told that a spare part was not available. Sanction for its procurement had been asked from the head office at Kolkata but had not come for the last six months. The cost of the part was about Rs. 35,000. Thus, for want of a sanction of Rs. 35,000, millions worth of production was being lost. General Bhagat ordered that the part be procured within 48 hours and the unit re-commissioned within a week. He accepted full responsibility for the decision and told the accounts department that if the audit objected to the purchase, they could deduct the amount from his salary. Needless to say, the plant was put on stream quickly. A new result oriented approach and enthusiasm crept into the organization and DVC quickly became one of the best run organizations. Unfortunately, the General died after about a year. Things slowly lapsed to the old state. There are many such examples where leadership made the difference.

## Conclusion

The economic objectives have to be decided by the government in power. People like the author can only try to build Public support in favor of some of the objectives.

The economic objectives are not going to be easy to achieve. Too many vested interests are likely to be hurt. Many of the actions are not politically savvy. The fear of loosing votes will deter our political leaders from taking hard decisions. They have been practicing compulsive populism for too long. But the actions are essential for the survival of the nation.

# 20

# Sharing Experiences

## There are Success Stories

There have been success stories in developing countries. Many developing countries and sometimes states or provinces of developing countries, NGO's and individuals have been able to come up with ideas to reduce poverty, improve health services and sanitation, increase literacy and education and improve the environment. There is a crying need that government servant, political leaders and other related groups come to know about these success stories, study them and adapt them to the extent possible to improve the pace of developments in their countries. The success stories touched upon in this chapter are by no means exhaustive. They essentially illustrate how efforts of individuals and governments of developing countries have improved the lives of their countrymen.

## Some Success Stories

### *The Grameen Bank, Bangladesh*

The Grameen Bank is a micro-finance organization and community development bank started in Bangladesh that makes small loans known as micro-credit to groups of poor people without collateral. The word "Grameen" means "of the village". The bank provided working capital to the poor who have skills that can be utilized. A group-based credit approach is applied which utilizes the peer-pressure within the group to ensure the borrowers follow credit discipline. Another distinctive feature of the bank's credit program is that a significant majority of its borrowers are women. The Grameen Bank was inspired by the Bangladesh famine of 1974. It can be traced back to 1976 when Professor Muhammad Yunus, a Fulbright scholar and Professor at University of Chittagong, launched a research project to examine the possibility of designing a credit delivery system to provide banking services targeted to the rural poor. In October 1983, the Grameen Bank Project was transformed into an independent bank by Government of Bangladesh. The organization and its founder, Muhammad Yunus, were jointly awarded the Nobel Peace Prize in 2006. It is often cited as a success story in micro-finance and serves as a model for institutions with similar philosophy world-wide. The Bank today continues to expand across the nation and still provides small loans to the rural poor. By 2006, Grameen Bank had over 2,100 branches. Its success has inspired similar projects in more than 40 countries around the world and has encouraged World Bank to finance Grameen Bank type schemes.

### *Making of a Model Village, Ralegaon Siddhi, Maharashtra, India*

Ralegan Siddhi was a backward village with hopeless social and economic problems till 1975. Economic pressures had driven Ralegaon villagers towards alcohol and liquor business. It was turned round by Baburao Hazare, affectionately known as Anna Hazare, a retired soldier who took voluntarily retirement in 1975. Hazare returned to his village and dedicated himself to work for the betterment of his village. He started with re-building the village temple. Since the temple represents the cultural heart of a community, Hazare felt that renovation of the temple with his own money would be the best way to demonstrate his unselfish motives and create an interest in his activities. Inspired by his selfless devotion, first the youth, then the rest of villagers slowly began to rally around him. He helped about two hundred villagers to get jobs in the Government employment schemes. He encouraged several others to join the army. But, finding employment for all villagers was not possible. Hazare realized that it was necessary to increase their agricultural output. The key to increasing agricultural output and improving economic conditions is conserving soil and harnessing water for irrigation. Hazare persuaded the villagers to undertake watershed development. In order to conserve soil and water by checking the run off, contour trenches were constructed along the hill slopes. Grass, shrubs and about 300,000 trees were planted throughout the village. This proved successful and the groundwater levels in the wells increased. The production of grain increased. The per capita income of the village shot up. Ralegaon experimented with drip irrigation in a big way. Papaya, lemon and chillies have been planted on a plot of eighty acres entirely irrigated by the drip irrigation system. However, cultivation of water-intensive crops like sugar cane was banned. Crops such as pulses, oilseeds and certain cash crops with low water requirements were grown. Another innovation tried was the "Grain Bank" which was started in 1983. Farmers who had surplus grain voluntarily donated grain to the "Grain Bank". Villagers who did not have enough grain could "borrow" grain from this bank. The idea was to ensure that no villager would have to borrow money to meet food requirements.

Milk production was promoted in Ralegaon as a secondary occupation. Purchase of new cattle and improvement of the existing breed with the help of artificial insemination resulted in an improvement in the cattle stock. This resulted in increase of Milk production from 100 liters in 1975 to around 2500 liters per day in 2000.

Once, the economic situation had improved, attention turned towards social and economical change. Anna Hazare and the youth group took up the issue of alcoholism. At a meeting conducted in the temple, the villagers resolved to close down the liquor dens and ban the drinking of alcohol in the village. Over thirty liquor brewing units were closed by their owners voluntarily. Those who did not succumb to social pressure were forced to close down their businesses, when the youth group smashed up their liquor dens. The owners could not complain as their business was illegal. Tobacco, cigarettes, "beedies" or Indian cigars is not sold in any shop at Ralegaon Siddhi.

Hazare laid emphasis on education. Ralegaon did not have local school. The drop-out rate was high, more so for girls, because of socio-economic and cultural reasons. A "Balwadi" or play school was started in 1976. Primary and secondary schools were also established. The first girl of Ralegaon Siddhi to pass School Leaving Certificate was in 1982. Now many of them are in good position. Ralegaon boasts of one hundred graduates and 250 people pursuing jobs outside the village. The people of Ralegaon have largely succeeded in eradicating social discrimination on the basis of caste. The dalits have been integrated into the social and economic life of the village.

Most rural poor get into a debt-trap as they have to incur heavy expenses at the time of marriage of their son or daughter. It is an undesirable practice but has almost become a social obligation. Ralegaon's people have started celebrating marriages collectively. The feast is held together with all arrangements being made by the village. From 1976 to 1986, four hundred and twenty-four marriages have been held under this system. Ralegaon Siddhi has become a progressive and prosperous village.

### *Sulabh International*

The Sulabh International Social Service Organization was founded by Dr. Bindeshwar Pathak in the year 1970. It is the largest nationally and internationally recognized pan-India social service outfit with 60,000 volunteers. It has developed a scavenging-free two-pit pour-flush toilet (Sulabh Shauchalaya) which is a safe and hygienic on site human waste disposal technology and a new concept of maintenance and construction of pay and use public toilets, popularly known as Sulabh complexes with bath, laundry and urinal and toilet facilities. The Sulabh technology has so far liberated 60,000 scavengers from the demeaning practice of physically cleaning and carrying human excreta. Sulabh has set up more than 7,500 pay and use community toilet complexes and about 1.2 million Sulabh Shauchalayas in private houses which together are being used by more than ten million people every day. This novel self-sustaining system has also helped in ending the uncivilized practice of open-air defecation to some extent. The United Nations Center for Human Settlements has recognized Sulabh's cost-effective and appropriate sanitation system as a global 'Urban Best Practice' at the Habitat-II conference held at Istanbul (Turkey), in June 1996. The Economic and Social Council of United Nations has granted Special Consultative Status to Sulabh in recognition of its outstanding service to mankind.

### Mid-day Meals Program

The Mid-day Meal Scheme is the popular name for the school meal program in India. It involves providing lunch free of cost to school-children on all working days. The key objectives of the program are protecting children from hunger, increasing school enrolment and attendance, improving mixing among children belonging to all castes, addressing malnutrition and social empowerment by providing employment to women. The program was introduced in a small scale in 1960s. But the first major thrust came in 1982 when the then Chief Minister of Tamil Nadu, India, decided to universalize the scheme for all children in government schools in primary classes. Later the program was expanded to cover all children up to class 10. Tamil Nadu's mid-day meal program is among the best known in the country. The scheme has been expanded to all parts of India after a landmark direction by the Supreme Court of India on November 28, 2001. The success of this scheme is illustrated by the tremendous increase in the school participation and completion rates in the state of Tamil Nadu. One hundred twenty million children are so far covered under the Mid-day Meal Scheme, which is the largest school lunch program in the world. Funding for this program is by the Government of India and has been enhanced from Rs. 30.10 billion to Rs. 48.13 billion in 2006-07.

A school meal program is now a standard welfare measure for school children in developing as well as developed nations. Even countries such as USA have it in many states. World Food Program, among other organizations, are involved in the program in many countries across the world.

### Cooperative Dairy Movement

Traditionally, private traders and middlemen controlled the marketing and distribution system of milk in India. These middlemen decided the prices and the off-take from the farmers.

As milk is perishable, producers were compelled to sell it for whatever they were offered. Often, they had to sell cream and "ghee" or melted butter at throw-away prices. The private traders made a killing. India ranked nowhere amongst milk producing countries in the world in 1946. Gradually, the milk producers, with inspiration from some nationalist leaders and a local farmer, freedom fighter and social worker Tribhovandas Patel, realized that the exploitation by the trader could be checked only if they marketed their milk themselves. Amul was the result of the realization that they could pool up their milk and work as a cooperative. Amul stands for Anand Milk-producers Union Limited is the first dairy cooperative movement in India. It was formed in 1946. By the end of 1948, more than 400 farmers joined it. The quantity of milk produced by one village cooperative increased from 250 to 5,000 liters a day. Dr. Verghese Kurien, a dairy technologist, volunteered to help Shri Tribhovandas Patel, in setting up a milk processing plant. The success of Amul was instrumental in launching the White Revolution that has made India the largest producer of milk and milk products in the world. The dairy movement in India is termed as Operation Flood. The breakthrough technology of spray-drying and processing buffalo milk, developed by Mr. H.M. Dalaya, was one of the key factors that contributed to the Revolution. The Amul model is followed with great success in many states of India. These dairies under the Dairy Development Board collect milk from collection points set up in different villages and make payments directly to village cooperatives. The milk so collected is processed, packed and marketed. Different milk products are prepared and sold.

### *Prime Minister's Rural Roads Development Program*

Rural Road Connectivity is a key component of Rural Development. It provides access to economic and social services to the village and thereby generates increased agricultural incomes and productive employment opportunities. Till 2000, about 40 per cent of the villages in the country were still not connected by all-weather roads. With a view to redress the situation, Government of India launched the Pradhan Mantri Gram Sadak Yojana (Prime Minister's Rural Roads Development

Program) on 25th December, 2000 to provide all-weather access to unconnected habitations. The Pradhan Mantri Gram Sadak Yojana (PMGSY) is a 100 per cent Centrally Sponsored Scheme. 50 per cent of the Cess on High Speed Diesel (HSD) is earmarked for this Program. Government of India is endeavoring to set high and uniform technical and management standards and facilitating policy development and planning at State level in order to ensure sustainable management of the rural roads network. In the first phase, habitations (hamlets) of population of 1000 (500 in the case of Hill States, Tribal and Desert areas) and above will be covered. In the second phase habitations of population of 500 (250 in the case of Hill States, Tribal and Desert areas) will be covered. About 368,000 km of new road construction and 370,000 km of upgrading/renewal is expected to be done at a cost of about $ 26 billion.

### *Mini/Micro Hydro-Electric Projects*

Like most developing countries, many villages in India are not connected to the national electricity grid. The problem is extremely acute in hilly and mountainous regions where erecting and maintaining distribution lines is difficult and very costly. The situation has been improved slightly by using eco-friendly water mills to generate enough power for a village. In Lachiwala village near Dehradun, one water mill upgraded at a cost of Rs. 10,000 generates enough electricity to light home appliances along with grinding grains. In another example in village Khod in Rudraprayag district of Garhwal was able to generate 5 MW of electricity for the village. Mr. Bhandari, the water mill owner, designed his own turbine and started generating power. Due to his excellent effort, all 51 houses of his village have access to electric light.

The success in generating electricity from water mills encouraged the Government of India to encourage mini and micro hydroelectric (hydel) projects. A mini and micro hydel project is one where the flow of the river is used for generation of electricity. Most of such hydel projects are isolated entities and could be effectively used to meet local energy requirements. However, the surplus from such plants could be resold to the main grid. The focus of the Small Hydro Power (SHP) program in India is on promoting commercial exploitation and active private sector participation. An estimated potential of about 15,000 MW of SHP exists in India. The Central Electricity Authority (CEA) has conducted a study for potential sites of SHPs of up to 15 MW in all states. The Ministry of Non-conventional Energy Sources (MNES) has a database of 4,096 potential sites with an aggregate capacity of 10,071 MW for projects up to 25 MW. In 1989, the total installed capacity of SHPs up to 3 MW capacity was only 63 MW. In just 10 years, this capacity has increased nearly four-fold to 226 MW. India has so far set up 387 SHPs of up to 25 MW capacity totaling 1,341.05 MW. These projects are spread throughout the country in hilly regions as well as on canal drops. One hundred and seventy projects of 25 MW with a total capacity of nearly 498.28 MW are under implementation. Most SHPs are grid-connected. However, there are some projects which are decentralized and are managed by local community organizations or NGOs. Thirteen states of India have announced their policies for private sector participation in the SHP sector. Thirty-five portable micro-hydel sets of up to 15 kW capacity have so far been installed in Uttar Pradesh, Bihar, West Bengal, J&K, Arunachal Pradesh and Himachal Pradesh. These sets are providing electricity to unelectrified villages and are being maintained by local communities.

Recently, a program on development and upgradation of water mills has been started by MNES. This would enable the direct use of mechanical power for different applications. MNES is also implementing a UNDP-GEF Hilly Hydro project in 13 states of Himalayan and Sub-Himalayan region. MNES has supported projects at 279 sites of which 54 were sanctioned in 2000 to undertake Detailed Survey and Investigation (DSI) and Detailed Project Reports (DPRs). Under its scheme of Capital Subsidy, MNES is supporting 91 Demonstration SHPs with an aggregate capacity of 143.23 MW spread over 22 states and Union Territories. So far, 36 projects aggregating 30.6 MW have been commissioned. Under this MNES has supported six SHPs aggregating 39.75 MW. MNES has launched a Demonstration Project to study the performance of portable micro-hydel sets under field conditions. Fifty portable micro-hydel sets of 5-15 kW capacity have been provided to local bodies/ communities in seven states. Of these, 41 sets have been installed. India has a well-established manufacturing base for a full range and type of SHP equipment. There are over eight manufacturers in the country in the field of SHP who are supplying various types of turbines, generators and control equipment.

## Conclusion

The problems of the developing countries are entirely different from developed countries. The developing countries have to learn from each other and formulate action plans based on their own strengths and weaknesses. However, we must remember the thought which is expressed by an advertisement of Kuwait Development Fund, "If you feed the hungry, he will be hungry again after four hours. If you can help him earn, he will feed himself and his family." Neo-liberal capitalism does not help the poor but developing countries cannot neglect their poor and must find strategies for inclusive growth.

# Epilogue

Today, the US is on the verge of recession. Europe expects only 2 per cent growth in foreseeable future if at all. The health of the developed world economies and particularly that of the US is critical for the developing countries to achieve their export driven growth strategies. Can one realistically hope for miracles? IMF predicts that the world economy will see a slow down in 2008. The world will possibly see a deeper, wider and a more prolonged downturn a little later. Jeffery Sachs, Director, Institute of International Development, Harvard, USA, says he thought this was a crisis of capitalism and not just Asian Capitalism. Market reforms IMF style have increased poverty and rich poor divide in most cases. Currency devaluations and economic reforms have not produced the desired results.

Today we are told by the developed world that the only system allowed is that of capitalist free market of globalization, privatization and consumerism and the developing countries must strengthen it by completing and signing the Doha Round of negotiations. Everyone must accept the system or be considered a heretic and punished accordingly. Are we only interested in the means and not the end? We are being told that the collapse of our economies, of our currencies, our industries is good for us in the long run. How do we tell our unemployed millions and closing companies that their misfortune is good for them? That eating Kellogg cornflakes and McDonalds Burgers, drinking Foster Beer and Scotch whiskey, using Revlon lipstick and riding

Mitsubishi Lancer represents consumer friendliness and benefits of globalization even if 80 per cent Indians have to satisfy themselves with watching the advertisements of these products while finding it difficult to ensure two square meals per day.

Developing nations including India have two options. They can follow the path of "Neo-liberal Capitalism", of unrestricted free market, of globalization, the so-called reform agenda of the G7 countries as dictated by World Bank or IMF as implemented through the WTO and see its rich get richer and poor getting poorer. They can watch with impotence the collapse of their currencies and economic and political enslavement by the developed world and their multinational corporations. Or they can discard this form of capitalism and follow a path of nationalism which will ensure a slow progress to prosperity, with lesser inequalities between the rich and the poor. They can follow a nationalism that shuns western consumerism and takes care of its people and the environment, a nationalism that ensures growth with humanity and cooperation as against mindless competition and conflict. They can opt for a nationalism that will ensure that India remains a free country and retains its economic and political sovereignty and is not ruled from Washington. A nationalism where profit is not the god but the Nation is. A nationalism where greed is not the sustaining religion but prudence is. They can follow a policy of nationalism which does not create destructive competition but which is tempered by humanity and cooperation.

Nationalism is not anti-west or anti-developed countries. If the economic interests of the western world were the same as that of the developed, there will be co-operation instead of conflict. Nationalism is guarding against western exploitation of our market in the guise of free market and reforms.

Nationalism is not revisionist. It is realist. It recognizes that there is a limit to export oriented growth. It is not possible for the developed world to totally absorb the entire exports of the developing world. The developing countries have to fight amongst themselves for a share of the market place. This is to the advantage of the developed world. Cheap import will always help them to keep inflation down. But this is disastrous to the developing world for some of them who cannot earn enough foreign exchange must accept economic enslavement. India can never earn its foreign exchange requirements through exports. Therefore, developing countries must control their imports.

Nationalism is neither communist nor even socialist. It does not promise cradle to grave welfare. But it does want that its people should all be above the poverty line. Nationalism believes that there should be social justice, humanity and co-operation. It also believes that, that is not possible in the capitalism that is practiced in the West. It does not believe that GDP (PPP) is an accurate measure of a nation's prosperity. If that was so, there should be no food riots in Indonesia whose per capita GDP (PPP) is over 3800 US dollars which work out to almost 10 US dollars per day or Rs. 420 per person per day. There should have been no persons below the poverty line in the United States which has a per capita GDP (PPP) of over 31,000 US dollars. But the United States has over 38 million citizen who live below their national poverty line. Fifteen million children in the United States are growing up in poverty. And the number is growing. The Neo-liberals may not care but Nationalist do care.

Nationalism is not against foreign investment. It is against foreign investment that would generate over capacities which in turn will result in an economic meltdown. It is against "Hot Money" which can disappear in hours if the so-called investor confidence is lost and create financial chaos. It is against foreign investment that comes with strings attached or that is forced upon the country for benefit of the developed world and their multinationals. Most world economists acknowledge the problem of hot money, and the damage it can do to the economic stability of a country.

Nationalism is not against privatization. It is against privatization of the profit making public sector units. It believes that countries and individuals do not get rich by selling performing assets. They get rich by selling non-performing assets and utilizing the receipts from the sale of these assets.

Nationalism is not against reducing government deficit. It is against distress selling of its assets to reduce this deficit. It is against reduction or elimination of subsidies which benefit its poor and protect its domestic industries from unfair competition and collapse. It seeks to reduce government deficit through generating income through taxing agricultural income, ensuring better tax compliance, closing down of loss making Public Sector Units and rooting out corruption.

Nationalism is not against profit. But profit is not its god and greed is not its religion. Nationalists salute their successful entrepreneurs. But they are against unethical business practices which aim to make money at the expense of the nation. It is against under invoicing of imports and over invoicing of exports. It is against its individuals stashing foreign currencies abroad. It is against all forms of tax and duty invasion.

Nationalism is not against the rich. It respects its rich for their honest enterprise and ability. It is against mindless western style consumerism which impoverishes the country through their demand for foreign imports. It is against western style consumerism for the degradation of the character of our youth and children and their criminalization to fulfill these urges.

Nationalism is not Jingoism. It supports world peace and good relationship with its neighbors on the basis of equality. But it is not willing to compromise on its national interests. It is willing to settle its existing border disputes with other countries on the basis of actual Line of Control. It seeks good relations with all countries on the basis of the UN Charter, on the basis of equality and non interference in the internal affairs of other countries. It does not accept usurping of our sovereignty by others.

Nationalism is not against economic reforms. It is against the market reforms as demanded by IMF. It has a different definition of economic reforms. It is against reforms as defined by the Washington Consensus of IMF, World Bank and the US Treasury. It is against reforms which forces us to adopt western consumerism or "Neo-liberal Capitalism". It is against reforms which open up our consumer goods market to foreign multinationals. It is against reforms which prevent us from controlling imports, private foreign borrowing and managing the current account balance and foreign exchange reserves. It is for ending the "licence raj". It is for reducing non-plan government spending. It is against privatization of the profit making Public Sector Units. It is for reforms which do not create mindless competition but reforms which enable growth with humanity, social justice and cooperation.

Nationalism stands for the right to choose. It is not an alien right. Every citizen of the developed countries enjoys this right. We want to be free to choose our form of government and our economic policies. We cannot be dictated by IMF or World Bank or WTO as to how we must conduct our trade and commerce or what is good for the Indian economy. We have the right to decide our own policies, to make mistakes and to learn from them. After all, IMF is not always right. Thirty-two of the 89 nations under its control have actually become poorer. The economies of 16 others have stagnated. It could not prevent the Asian meltdown. It could not prevent the collapse of the Russian economy or that of the Brazilian currency.

Nationalism does not believe in unrealistic ambition and baseless optimism. The Dow Jones crossed the 14,000 mark in 2007. That does not mean that everything is perfect in the world economy. It could mean that with the withdrawal of billions of dollars from the developing world and their investment in the US stock market has created the situation of too much money chasing too few shares. It is not a new situation for us. We have seen stock prices go through the roof in 1992 and 1995. It was too good to last. And when the prices crashed, it hurt too many investors. US stock markets have crashed in 2008 by 40 per cent and more. Many Fortune 500 companies have gone bankrupt.

Nationalism does not believe in unsustainable growth. The Asian Tigers achieved almost double digit growth for a few years through the unrestricted flow of foreign capital from the developed world. This money was used to build real-estate and factories leading to over production. Buildings remained unsold. Factory products piled up in warehouses. In the face of mounting debt the economies collapsed. Nationalism believes in a steady growth without too much foreign investment, a growth rate that can be maintained for the next fifty years.

Nationalists believe that successful management of foreign exchange reserves and the trade deficit is the key to financial stability of the country. They believe that foreign debt should be less than the foreign exchange reserve of the country. It believes that the country must import less than it exports in dollar terms. Only then can our foreign debt be controlled and slowly reduced. It is totally against import of consumer goods from the developed countries into India.

Nationalists believe that WTO is an unfair organization and any agreement signed in this regard is an unequal treaty and must therefore be abrogated at the earliest possible. Nationalists would like to follow the Chinese example of adopting the free market reforms and opening up of the economy to areas which are in our national interest and deny access to areas which are not in our interest. Russia is not a member of the WTO. That does not prevent the developed countries from trading with it. Countries, where profit is god and greed the sustaining religion, will trade with any country, whether member of WTO or not, as long as there is profit to be made. India is the second largest emerging market in the world. We must believe in our potential and our strengths. No country in the world can ignore India.

Indian Nationalism stands for a strong India, a prosperous India. It is proud of its culture and its heritage. It stands for a strong Rupee because it believes that a strong Rupee is more beneficial to its prosperity than a weak Rupee. It values its independence and is prepared to fight and struggle for its political and economic sovereignty. It does not like to be told what is good for us. It believes in doing its own thing and learn from its mistakes. It is willing to co-operate with nations who respect its sovereignty and are ready to co-operate on equal terms. It will resist exploitation by the strong and try to help out the week.

Developing countries are young nations weakened by centuries of colonization and exploitation. They are economic flyweights. They cannot survive free competition from the economic heavy weights, the G7 nations and their multinationals. They must therefore resist competition on equal terms and take protective measures as deemed necessary to keep unfair competition away from our economy. Give us another hundred years or perhaps even fifty. We will be more than ready to compete on equal terms.

It was the Nationalists who brought independence to India. Many of our social elite wanted us to remain a British colony. Mahatma Gandhi was a Nationalist. He wanted us to stop using foreign goods and to use Indian products. Subhash Chandra Bose was a Nationalist. He was not afraid to fight the might of the British Empire. Sardar Patel was a Nationalist. He brought the princely states into the Indian Union and gave India its present shape. Veer Savarkar was a Nationalist. He stood for the Indian culture. Lal Bahadur Shastri was a Nationalist. He commenced the green revolution and freed India from foreign dependence for food. Unfortunately Mrs. Indira Gandhi was the last Nationalist. She nationalized the banks and insurance and restricted the influence of the multinationals. She stood for self-reliance as the core policy. Nationalism seems to have died with her.

We, the Nationalist in India, are small in numbers. The nation is our God and prudence is our religion. We seek upliftment of all people of our nation and not only the urban rich. Our voice is weak and almost drowned in the chorus of self-seekers yelling for privatization, globalization and free market reforms in the media. We have our opponents in the Congress and the BJP (I wish and pray that the other parties cease to exist). We have our opponents in the intelligentsia, in our government, in the bureaucracy, in the industry and in foreign governments who want to see India cut to size. But we have faith. We believe that in the end truth will prevail. That is our sustaining religion. We believe India has the potential and the resources to be great, to prosper and be a world leader. We believe in our victory. We are not unique. Nationalists of all countries are the same.

What developing countries need are real leaders. They need leaders, who love their country and its sovereignty; leaders who are not afraid of bullies; leaders who are not afraid of privation and difficulties; leaders who will not sell their country or their freedom for a few dollars more. We need leaders like Saddam Hussein and Milosovich who believe in fighting for sovereignty. We need leaders like President Putin of Russia who can stand up to the US. We need leaders who believe in the strengths of their country and have the courage to fight against injustice, leaders who can fight to preserve our freedom.

It appears that leaders of most developing countries including India have opted for the soft approach. They want to follow Neo-liberal Capitalism rather than Nationalism. The begging bowls are out. Second generation reforms are in. Any measure, whether in the long-term interest of the country or otherwise, will be adopted to attract foreign investment.

May God save the developing countries from economic enslavement by developed countries and their multinational corporations.

# Bibliography


## Part I—Developing Nations and their Problems

**Chapter 1: Wealth and Prosperity**

en.wikepedia.org/wiki/world_economy

**Chapter 2: The Developed and the Developing World**

en.wikepedia.org/wiki/world_economy

en.wikipedia.org/wiki/developing countries

en.wikipedia.org/wiki/developed countries

www.economist.com

**Chapter 3: Feasibility of Export Oriented Growth**

en.wikepedia.org/wiki/world_economy

www.worldbank.org

Asia's Agony by Tony Emmerson, *Newsweek*, October 12, 1998

Editorial, Hold the Garbage, Thanks, *Asiaweek*, January 15, 1999

The Long, Hard Climb Back Up by Alejandro Reeves, *Asiaweek*, January 8, 1999.

www.economist.com

**Chapter 4: IMF and the Developing World**

en.wikepedia.org/wiki/world_economy

Free-Market Failures by Sadruddin Aga Khan, *Newsweek*, October 12, 1998

Heads Down by Velisarios Kattoulas, *Newsweek*, October 12, 1998

Reform's Trials by Tim Healy, *Asiaweek*, January 15, 1999

Grumbles from the Left by Todd Crowell and David Hseih, *Asiaweek*, January 15, 1999

Reform is Crucial, message from IMF Dy Managing Director, *Asiaweek*, January 8, 1999

**Chapter 5: WTO and the Developing World**

en.wikepedia.org/wiki/world_economy

www.wto.org

www.economist.com

**Chapter 6: Foreign Investment and the Developing Countries**

en.wikepedia.org/wiki/world_economy

www.economist.com

**Chapter 7: Multinationals and the Developing World**

en.wikepedia.org/wiki/world_economy

www.corporations.org

**Chapter 8: Inflation and the Developing World**

en.wikepedia.org/wiki/world_economy

**Chapter 9: Foreign Exchange Management and the Developing World**

en.wikepedia.org/wiki/world_economy

www.economist.com

**Chapter 10: Consumerism and the Developing Countries**

en.wikepedia.org/wiki/world_economy

**Chapter 11: Subsidies and the Developing World**

en.wikepedia.org/wiki/world_economy

www.economist.com

**Chapter 12: Poverty and the Third World**

en.wikepedia.org/wiki/world_economy

"The Other America" by Jonathan Alter, *Newsweek*, 19 September 2005

**Chapter 13: Globalization and Developing Countries**

en.wikepedia.org/wiki/world_economy

www.bls.gov

www.topics.mytimes.com

Letters to the Editor, *Newsweek*, October 12, 1998

The Crash of 99? by Robert J. Samuelson, *Newsweek*, October 12, 1998

Coming Apart by Michael Elliot, *Newsweek*, October 12, 1998

Everybody Free Up Please: Interview, Sir Leon Brittan, The World in 1998, *The Economist*

Housing Meltdown Hits US Economy by Steve Schifferes, Economic Reporter, BBC News

## Part II—Models for Development

**Chapter 14: Capitalism**

en.wikepedia.org/wiki/world_economy

Capitalism in Crisis by Robert J. Samuelson, *Newsweek*, September 14, 1998

en.wikepedia.org/wiki/world_economy

**Chapter 15: Communism**

en.wikepedia.org/wiki/world_economy

www.communism.org

**Chapter 16: Socialism**

en.wikepedia.org/wiki/world_economy

**Chapter 17: Concept of Nationalism**

## Part III—Implementation of Nationalism

**Chapter 18: A Swot Analysis on India**

Promise and Pitfalls by Rohit Saran and Shefali Rekhi, *India Today*, March 3, 1999

We, The Wretched: Cover Story, *Outlook*, August 13, 1997

**Chapter 19: Economic Objectives and Analysis of Options**

**Chapter 20: Sharing Experiences**

en.wikepedia.org/wiki/world_economy

# Index